RIGHTING CANADA'S WRONGS

Residential Schools
The Devastating Impact on Canada's Indigenous Peoples and the Truth and Reconciliation Commission's Findings and Calls for Action

Melanie Florence

JAMES LORIMER & COMPANY LTD., PUBLISHERS
TORONTO

James Lorimer & Company Ltd., Publishers
acknowledges the support of the Ontario Arts
Council. We acknowledge the support of the
Canada Council for the Arts, which last year
invested $24.3 million in writing and publishing
throughout Canada. We acknowledge the
Government of Ontario through the Ontario Media
Development Corporation's Ontario Book Initiative.

Library and Archives Canada Cataloguing in
Publication

Florence, Melanie, author
        Residential schools : the devastating impact
on Canada's Indigenous Peoples and the Truth and
Reconciliation Commission's findings and calls for
action / Melanie Florence.

(Righting Canada's wrongs)
Includes bibliographical references and index.
ISBN 978-1-4594-0866-1 (bound)

        1. Native peoples—Canada—Residential
schools—Juvenile literature. I. Title.
II. Series: Righting Canada's wrongs

E96.5.F56 2016   j371.829'97071
C2014-907550-2

James Lorimer & Company Ltd., Publishers
317 Adelaide Street West, Suite 1002
Toronto, ON, Canada
M5V 1P9
www.lorimer.ca

Printed and bound in Canada.
Manufactured by Friesens Corporation in Altona,
Manitoba, Canada in March 2016.
Job #221527

Also in the Righting Canada's Wrongs series

The Chinese Head Tax
*and Anti-Chinese Immigration
Policies in the Twentieth Century*

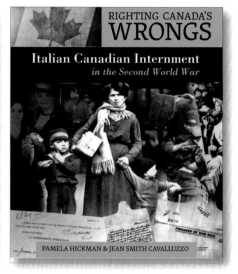

**Italian Canadian
Internment**
in the Second World War

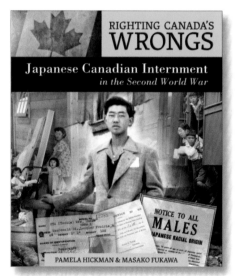

**Japanese Canadian
Internment**
in the Second World War

The Komagata Maru
*and Canada's Anti-Indian
Immigration Policies in the
Twentieth Century*

Contents

MAP OF RESIDENTIAL SCHOOLS 4

INTRODUCTION 7

LIFE BEFORE THE SCHOOLS
Aboriginal Diversity 8
Food and Medicine 12
Clothing, Shelter, and Transportation 16
Trade Goods 20
Family, Community, Language, Culture,
and Religion 24
Educating the Children 32

CONFLICT ARISING FROM CONTACT
Crown and Aboriginal Sovereignties 38
Assimilation: A Government Policy 42
Assimilation Policy and Practice 44
Cutting Cultural Ties 46

THE CHILDREN ARE TAKEN
Forced Removal 48
Separation 50

LIFE AT RESIDENTIAL SCHOOL
Shock 54
Starvation 58
Education in English and French 60
Child Labour 66
The Inuit Schools 68
Abuse 72
Some Good Memories 76
Runaways and Death at School 80

CLOSING THE SCHOOLS
A Failing Grade 82
Closing the Doors 84

LIFE AFTER RESIDENTIAL SCHOOL
The Struggle of Survivors 86
The Next Generations 90
Speaking Out 94
Survivors as Leaders 96

APOLOGY AND REDRESS
The Government Apologizes 98
The Churches Apologize 104
The Truth and Reconciliation Commission 106
Coming to Terms with Our History 110
Calls to Action 112
Understanding — and Action: Next Steps 116
Permanent Acknowledgements 118

Timeline 120

Glossary 122

For Further Reading 124

Visual Credits 125

Index 127

WATCH THE VIDEO

Look for this symbol throughout the book for links to video and audio clips available online.

Visit www.lorimer.ca/wrongs to see the entire series

Map of Residential Schools

This map shows the location of residential schools identified by the Indian Residential Schools Settlement Agreement.

Shingle Point

Inuvik Grollier Hall
Inuvik Stringer Hall

Aklavik All Saints
Aklavik Immaculate Conception

Fort McPherson

Federal Hostel-Cambridge Bay

St. Pauls Holstel

Yukon

Whitehorse Baptist

Yukon Hall

Coudert Hall

Carcross

Coppermine

Federal Hostel-Fort Franklin

Northwest Territories

Nunavut

Fort Simpson Bompas Hall

Fort Simpson Lapointe Hall

Lower Post

Akaitcho Hall

Fort Resolution

Fort Providence

Federal Hostel Baker Lake/ Qamani'tuaq

Hay River

Fort Smith Breynat Hall
Fort Smith Grandin College

Port Simpson

Kitimaat

Assumption

Holy Angels

Fort Vermillon

Federal Hostel-Eskimo Point/ Arviat

British Columbia

Alberta

Lejac

St. Augustine

Whitefish Lake

Desmarais Wabasca

Manitoba

St. Michael's

Anahim

Joussard

Grouard
Lesser Slave Lake

Saskatchewan

Beauval

Guy Hill

Cariboo

Sturgeon Lake

Edmonton
St. Albert

Blue Quills

Lac La Ronge

Mackay - The Pas

Ahousat

Sechelt

Ermineskin

Lac la Biche

Onion Lake
St. Anthony's

Sturgeon Landing

Norway

Christie

St. Paul's

Kamloops

Morely

Sarcee

Thunderchild

Prince Albert

Pine Creek

Mackay - Dauphin

Alberni

St. George's

St. Joseph's

Old Sun

St. Michael's

Sandy Bay

Cranbrook

Fort Pelly
St. Phillip's
Crowstand
Cote

Birtle

Fort Alexander

Coqualeetza

Crowfoot

Battleford

Kuper Island

Sacred Heart
St. Cyprian's

Portage la Prairie

Assinibo

St. Mary's

St. Paul's
St. Mary's

Regina

File Hills

Round Lake

Elkhorn

Gordon's

Lebret

Brandon

Muscowequan

Marieval

Federal Hostel-
Pond Inlet/
Mittimatalik

Federal Hostel-
Broughton Island/
Qikiqtarjuaq

Federal Hostel-
Pangnirtung

Federal Hostel-
Igloolik/Iglulik

Federal Hostel-
Frobisher Bay

Federal Hostel-
Cape Dorset/
Kinngait

Federal Hostel-
Lake Harbour

Chesterfield Inlet

Federal Hostel-
Payne Bay

Federal Hostel-
George River

Canada

Federal Hostel-
Port Harrison

Churchill Vocational Centre

Federal Hostel-
Belcher Islands

Newfoundland
& Labrador

Cross Lake

Federal Hostel-
Great Whale River

House

Fort George (St. Phillip's)
Fort George (St. Joesph's)
Fort George Hostels

Ontario

St. Anne's

Quebec

Newfoundland
& Labrador

Poplar Hill

Amos

Sept-Iles

er

Point Bleue

McIntosh

Pelican Lake

Bisphop
Horden Hall

New
Brunswick

P.E.I

St. Mary's
Cecilla Jeffery

Fort William

oia

La Tuque

Shubenacadie

Fort Frances

Chapleau

Spanish Boys' School
Spanish Girls' School

Nova Scotia

Shingwauk
Wawanosh Home

Mohawk Institute

Mount Elgin

To my grandfather, who survived.
And always, for Joshua and Taylor.

Introduction

As a result of the work of the Truth and Reconciliation Commission, Canadians are now much more aware of the facts regarding residential schools and the impact of this system on generations of Aboriginal people in Canada. The Commission's final report made numerous recommendations, including that non–Indigenous Canadians be more fully educated on this topic.

One of the Commission's calls to action states: "Make age-appropriate curriculum on residential schools, Treaties, and Aboriginal peoples' historical and contemporary contributions to Canada a mandatory education requirement for Kindergarten to Grade Twelve students."

This book makes extensive use of the information and analysis provided in the Commission's report and addresses difficult topics that, up until now, have not been fully dealt with in Canadian schools. It is my hope that this book will be useful for the education of Canadians by helping to make those topics more accessible and sparking some long overdue discussions.

Truth and Reconciliation Commissioner Marie Wilson explained the importance of the Commission's initiative: "Think about your Canadian history classes. Did the story of Canada begin only shortly before Europeans came up the river [Ottawa] is built on? How honest are our textbooks about the traditional keepers of their land and their part in Canada's story? How frank and truthful are we with Canadian students about the history of residential schools and the role our governments and religious institutions played in its systematic attempt to erase the cultures of aboriginal people?"

Justice Murray Sinclair, the chair of the Commission, put it this way on the day the final report was released: "Reconciliation is not an aboriginal problem — it is a Canadian problem. It involves all of us."

— Melanie Florence

CHAPTER 1

LIFE BEFORE THE SCHOOLS

Aboriginal Diversity

For thousands of years before European settlers arrived, Aboriginal peoples lived rich and full lives, steeped in tradition and ceremony. The First Nations population in Canada has always been a diverse one, often divided by historians into six distinct groups based on geographical location. Each lived according to what the land provided. Some, such as the Pacific Coast First Nations, lived in permanent settlements of log homes and ate a diet of mainly fish and seafood. Others, such as the Woodland First Nations of central Canada, were nomadic, seasonally following the animals that they hunted and trapped. They traditionally lived in tipis that could easily be put up or taken down and transported from place to place. In addition to the First Nations were the Inuit, formerly called Eskimos, who lived in the Far North of Canada. Their culture and survival were also shaped by the natural environment around them. Despite differences in lifestyle, language, food, and dress, there were many similarities among First Nations and Inuit peoples.

Woodland First Nations

Woodland First Nations were made up of many smaller groups. They lived in the boreal forests of the central and eastern parts of the country. The Woodland peoples were hunters who migrated, following the animals that they hunted. They used spears and bows and trapped in their own distinct territories.

Mi'kmaq

The Mi'kmaq inhabited the Atlantic region of Canada. They spent the warmer spring and summer months on the coast, fishing and hunting and sometimes going out to sea in search of whales. In the fall and winter, they moved inland and settled near smaller bodies of water where they could hunt, fish, and trap.

Plains First Nations

The Plains First Nations lived on the grasslands of the Prairies. They lived as migratory groups. They gathered together in the summer for feasts, ceremonies, and to hunt. These hunts provided buffalo meat and hides for the remainder of the year.

Iroquoian First Nations

The Iroquoian First Nations practised agriculture in the southernmost part of what is now Canada. They lived in permanent locations. The fertile land was perfect for growing crops and for hunting, which allowed them to build thriving democratic communities. They lived in longhouses and the women headed their families.

Mackenzie and Yukon River Basin First Nations

Survival was challenging for this group. They lived in barren, swampy areas. Community leaders were chosen based on who could provide for them. Hunters were greatly revered because there was little game to be had. Winters were harsh and groups kept to their own territory to hunt. Homes had to be portable so that each group could pack up and relocate easily to follow their food source.

Pacific Coast First Nations

The Pacific Coast First Nations had rich food sources, including salmon, shellfish, and other seafood. Their permanent homes were made from the huge red cedars that grew locally. The homes were large and several families could live together. They had a distinct social system and aristocracy.

Inuit

The Inuit, formerly called Eskimos, live in northern Canada and have a distinct language and culture. Traditionally, the Inuit survived on hunting and fishing.

Northern Peoples

Ice fishing, pictured above, provided Inuit peoples with one of the staples of their diet. This Inuit man is dressed in traditional clothing made of animal skins and fur.

Metis

Although the Hudson's Bay Company initially banned the interracial marriages of European men and Aboriginal women, they eventually accepted them. Contracts, such as this one from 1837, made these marriages legal. The children of these unions were called Metis.

Who Are the Metis?

The first Metis, from the French word for "mixed," were the children of European fishermen and their Native wives. Later, the Metis were the children of French-Canadian fur traders who married Aboriginal women. Considered to be neither European nor Aboriginal, the Metis developed their own lifestyle and culture, which combined both sides of their heritage. Metis people were mostly located on the Canadian fur trade routes.

The Metis developed their own lifestyle and culture, which combined both sides of their heritage.

Metis Family

Metis children were usually raised in their mothers' cultures and many lived in their Indigenous communities. Metis women translated for their trapper husbands and shared their knowledge of the land and customs of their people.

Food and Medicine

Aboriginal peoples lived off the land successfully for generations before colonization. Hunting, trapping, and fishing provided meat. The Iroquoian First Nations grew crops, especially corn, beans, and squash, known as "The Three Sisters." They and others also gathered local wild plants for food and medicines. Wild rice, mushrooms, and many other plants supplemented what the First Nations could grow or hunt.

Moose
Woodland First Nations peoples used moose for meat as well as the hide to make clothing. A large bull could provide a group with more than 200 kilograms of meat and fat.

Farming
The Iroquoian First Nations peoples grew crops that were eaten fresh or dried for food during the winter. Corn was ground into meal or flour and used in many dishes.

Wild Rice

Wild rice is a kind of marsh grass. Canoes were used to harvest the seeds, which formed an important part of the diet of many groups.

First Nations people taught the settlers how to tap trees and make maple syrup and sugar.

Maple Sugar and Syrup

An Iroquoian legend tells of the discovery of maple syrup when a chief pulled an axe out of a sugar maple tree and left for the day to hunt. The sap dripped out of the tree and into a birchbark bowl. His wife discovered it and, thinking it was water, made a venison stew. The boiling process created maple syrup. The birchbark containers shown here would hold and store the sugar, while the skimmer would be used during the boiling process. First Nations people taught the settlers how to tap trees and make maple syrup and sugar. The sap of birch trees was also used to make syrup.

Fish
Nuu-chah-nulth women are shown processing halibut at Neah Bay, British Columbia. Coastal peoples ate a diet consisting primarily of halibut and salmon. Just a few weeks of dedicated fishing yielded enough fish to feed a clan for the year and to trade for goods.

Sage and Sweat Lodges
This image shows the frame of a sweat lodge with a pile of sage inside. The frame would be covered to trap the heat and smoke of the burning sage. Sage is one of the sacred medicines that Aboriginal peoples relied on for healing. It represented strength and wisdom and was often used to purify a place or a person of negative energy.

Plants for Food and Medicine
Aboriginal peoples and their healers believed that every tree, shrub, and flower had a use and was given to them by the Creator. Roots and berries could be gathered and used for food, but through trial and error healers found medicinal uses for plants as well. This knowledge was passed down through generations within a community. Aboriginal peoples were generally healthy but European explorers, traders, and settlers brought with them very debilitating diseases, such as smallpox, that were previously unknown to the area.

Medicine Bundle
Traditional medicines were often made from dried roots, leaves, and other plant parts and formed into small bundles like this one. Different mixes of plants would be used for a variety of injuries or ailments.

Starvation

After traders and settlers arrived, Canada's western prairies and forests were over-hunted and the animals that Native peoples relied on for food became scarce and sometimes disappeared. The buffalo population was severely depleted and deer and other large game were much less plentiful. Aboriginal peoples experienced starvation. Their traditional ways of life were undermined. Some resorted to begging for food from the settlers, as shown in this illustration. Historians have documented the use of starvation as a tool by the Canadian government in the West to force First Nations peoples to agree to treaties and to move onto reserves.

"This is our land! It isn't just a piece of pemmican to be cut off and given in little pieces back to us."

— Chief Poundmaker

Hardship

Due to the drastic decline of the buffalo and other wildlife populations and low prices for furs, the Plains Cree (shown here around 1880) suffered serious hardship. Cree Chief Poundmaker resisted signing land treaties that would force them to leave their land and move onto a reserve, saying, "This is our land! It isn't just a piece of pemmican to be cut off and given in little pieces back to us. It is ours and we will take what we want."

Clothing, Shelter, and Transportation

Clothing, shelter, and transportation varied greatly among First Nations and Inuit peoples. If a group was migratory, their homes had to be light and mobile. If the group lived full-time near their food source, they built more permanent houses. Some First Nations travelled by canoe, while others used dogsleds or horses. Clothing varied by region and also by use. There was everyday clothing as well as ceremonial regalia.

Ceremonial Shoes
Specific kinds of clothing were worn for different ceremonies. Beaded moccasins with ankle bells, shown here, were worn as part of the traditional costume during the Sun Dance ceremony on the Blood Indian Reserve near Cardston, Alberta.

Traditional Clothes
This First Nations man and his child are dressed traditionally in clothing made of fur and hides. Both people are wearing moccasins, which are soft shoes made from the skins of animals. Clothes were often decorated with intricate beading. Clothes were also made from cloth that was woven from plant material, or that was purchased through trade.

War Bonnets
War bonnets featured features from eagles, the fiercest of birds. They were generally worn by chiefs. An eagle feather could also be earned by children when they put the community before themselves. The feather was awarded in front of the entire community.

Dogs

Survival often depended on creative use of available natural resources. The Salish of the West Coast, pictured above, used dog wool for weaving shawls and blankets. These women are wearing skirts made from bark.

A Cree Lodge

This depiction of the interior of a Cree lodge was drawn by Robert Hood during an expedition to the Coppermine River in the Northwest Territories from 1819 to 1821. By the time of Hood's visit, the western Cree had been involved in the European fur trade for more than 150 years. Note the metal pot, which made it much easier for women to prepare food over the fire.

The Significance of Hair

Long hair was considered sacred. The more pure your thoughts were, the longer, healthier, and more vibrant your hair would be. Hair could be braided with the three pieces of the braid representing body, mind, and spirit. Often, hair was cut only during mourning. It represented a cutting off of the past and a new beginning.

Shelter

Different nations with different resources and ways of life required different types of homes. Groups that migrated with the hunt lived in tipis, seen here, that could be taken down and transported with them when they moved from place to place.

Shelter for Metis Families
The Metis lived in log homes, following European customs for building houses. This drawing shows the interior of a Metis house in 1874. Before the influx of settlers in the 1870s, many Metis families prospered by combining commercial buffalo hunting, trading, carting, farming, and working as seasonal employees of the Hudson's Bay Company, which operated over a vast territory in western and northern Canada.

Birchbark Canoes
Aboriginal peoples used the resources around them in their everyday lives. Each nation relied on different materials and foods for survival. These Ojibwa women are shown mending a birchbark canoe in Northwest Angle, Minnesota, in 1872. Canoes were essential to transportation through the local waterways. Typically, a single piece of birchbark that was five to six metres long and one to two metres wide was used. Bark was used for a variety of purposes, including covering tipis, as seen in the background. This practice continued long after the introduction of European goods through the fur trade.

Sleds
These Inuit children are sitting on a komatik, or sled. Sleds made transportation in the snow and ice much easier. They could be pulled by dogs.

Horses
For hundreds of years, Aboriginal peoples walked from place to place. Then they began training wild horses for riding. Horses were also used to pull heavy loads.

Kayaks
The Inuit invented the kayak, seen here. It was traditionally a single-person boat propelled by a double-bladed paddle. Kayaks were used for transportation and hunting. The shape of the kayak allowed a hunter to move silently through the water.

Sled Dogs
Dogs were raised and trained by Inuit to pull sleds across ice and snow. The sleds would be used to carry loads of wood or provisions while the Inuit would usually walk behind.

Clothing, Shelter, and Transportation

Trade Goods

Selling furs to traders gave Aboriginal peoples access to goods that had been previously unavailable to them, such as guns and fabric. While the impact of introducing most of these trade goods was positive, there were some goods such as alcohol that brought very negative results.

Trading also benefited the colonists. European demand for furs, particularly beaver, was high and the fur trade gave profitable access to these furs. The fur trade was the source of much of the early contact between traders and Aboriginal peoples.

Fish Trade
Pacific Coast First Nations harvested salmon, herring, crab, and other shellfish. Before contact, they engaged in extensive inter-nation trading of fish and fish products. After contact, they also sold fish to European fur traders and colonists.

Trading Food
Beginning in the late eighteenth century, fur traders built a string of posts along the edge of the grasslands to gain access to pemmican and other provisions that Plains buffalo hunters provided. This 1848 painting by Paul Kane shows Cree or Assiniboine lodges in front of Rocky Mountain Fort, British Columbia.

Furs
Hudson's Bay Company employees are seen here at a portage transporting furs from Lake Winnipeg to York Factory, Manitoba.

Trading in the North
In this photo, a group of Inuit show a fur trader an Arctic fox skin at the Revillon Frères post at Cape Dufferin, Quebec. Aboriginal peoples sold furs in exchange for guns, iron utensils, fabric, tea, and alcohol.

Some goods such as alcohol brought very negative results.

Making Trades
This painting shows an Aboriginal family trading furs for guns and other goods. Guns made hunting easier so more animals could be taken. That, combined with the increase in settlers who also relied on hunting, caused wildlife populations to decrease dramatically.

Trade Goods 21

Weapons for the Hunt
These Iroquois in traditional clothing are posed for the camera. They show off both rifles and traditional weapons, such as bows and arrows, used for hunting.

Blankets, weapons, metal tools, pots, and alcohol were items that Aboriginal people commonly traded for during the eighteenth and nineteenth centuries.

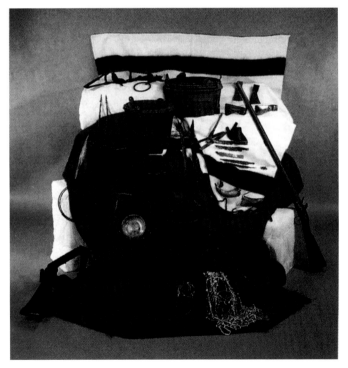

Trade Goods
Blankets, weapons, metal tools, pots, and alcohol were items that Aboriginal peoples commonly traded for during the eighteenth and nineteenth centuries. They also traded for European-style clothing and fabric.

Two-Way Trade
This collection of trade articles is from around 1870. Both sides of the fur trade placed high value on the goods available. Europeans prized the furs, as well as leather clothing and goods; beaded items; decorative items, such as birchbark boxes adorned with porcupine quills; and beautiful baskets woven from a variety of plant materials.

Gold Prospectors
Learning from the white miners, Aboriginals made most of the major gold discoveries in the Canadian West during the latter half of the nineteenth century. They mined gold by panning, and then learned how European miners used sluices to mine more gold faster. These First Nations men and women are placer-gold miners on the Thompson River, British Columbia.

Family, Community, Language, Culture, and Religion

While Aboriginal peoples had many distinct languages and dialects that set them apart from one another, the sense of community and focus on their families was something they all shared. Although they had differences, they shared similar cultural practices and religious ceremonies, such as traditional dance. Shortly after the early explorers arrived, missionaries came to introduce Christianity to the Native peoples. Their early influence had a big impact on the future relationship between the churches and Aboriginal peoples across Canada.

Keeping Baby Close
Babies were often strapped onto cradleboards, which protected them and kept them close to their mothers. A cradleboard was typically used for the first few months of an infant's life, when the mother would carry the baby around with her. Mothers would sometimes hang dreamcatchers or beaded amulets to keep the babies amused while they went about their daily routine.

The Family Unit
Aboriginal families encompassed more than just the nuclear family. For First Nations peoples, Metis (pictured here), and Inuit, the family was the community as a whole. Everyone had some responsibility in raising and educating the children.

Unusual Pets

In this photo, an Aboriginal boy has some unusual pets — a young fox and a beaver. Children were taught to respect Mother Earth and all her creatures. Although children learned to hunt early by playing games with toy bows and arrows, animals were hunted for food, not for sport. Thanks were given for the animal's sacrifice.

Children were highly valued, greatly loved members of the community.

Children

Children were highly valued, greatly loved members of the community. Note how the clothing was designed to carry the baby on the mother's back.

Family, Community, Language, Culture, and Religion

Clans

This mask was most likely worn by a member of the Bear clan of the Tsimshian Nation, which is one of the most prominent First Nations clans on the West Coast. Clans were often named after animals, such as Wolf and Raven, and were arranged in a hierarchy of importance.

Iroquoian Council

Iroquoian chiefs were chosen by the elder women of the Nation, who were highly respected. Traditionally, children in Iroquoian First Nations were born into their mothers' clans and not the clans of their fathers. This painting depicts an Iroquoian council fire and a discussion with a European man.

Ceremonial Dancing

Aboriginal children were encouraged to participate in ceremonies, including dances. Ceremonies, whether in a sweat lodge or at a powwow, were usually conducted in a circle. The circle represented life and how each person was on a circular journey throughout it. This illustration shows the dance of the Kutcha-Kutchi of the Yukon and Lower Mackenzie valleys.

Totem Poles

Totem poles were traditional symbols on the West Coast. They were carved from the huge red cedar trees found there. Figures could represent sacred animals or characters from Native legends and represented clan lineages or specific events. They were also used to mark the family living in a house or as tomb markers.

Amulets

This beaded turtle amulet was used in a girl's puberty ceremony. It symbolized procreation, which was then explained to the girl. Puberty was celebrated in many different Native cultures. Women were often secluded and some Native men were sent on a vision quest.

Powwow

Traditionally, powwows were held to give the Native people an opportunity to trade, share celebrations, and to allow warriors to re-enact their battles or hunts for everyone to witness. The closest English language translation of the word powwow is "meeting."

Aboriginal children were encouraged to participate in ceremonies, including dances.

Sun Dance

The Sun Dance was a ritual where participants pledged to fast and exert themselves to obtain spiritual power or to fulfill a vow. The ritual could include piercing and attaching something heavy to hang from the skin.

Language Development

Children grew up learning the specific language spoken in their community. Language is a vital link to a person's culture, so passing on a traditional dialect was essential in helping to keep their culture alive. Their parents and all community members would help teach the youth about their heritage and culture.

Potlatch

Potlatch was a ceremony that brought many groups in the Pacific Northwest together to celebrate life events such as births, deaths, marriages, naming ceremonies, and appointing a new chief. Storytelling and dancing were integral parts of a potlatch. Hosts would often give away their possessions to thank guests for witnessing the ceremony. Settlers enjoyed the colourful and exciting ceremonies. A crowd of them are visible on the bridge watching from above.

Artwork

The styles and materials used in traditional crafts were associated with particular nations or subgroups. They were used for trade amongst Aboriginal peoples as well as trade with Europeans. West Coast button blankets like this one were highly prized as trade items and showed traditional symbols of plants and animals in the surrounding environment.

Dance

This contemporary photo shows a Shoshone traditional dance.

Drumming

Drums were often used in ceremonies where there was singing and dancing. The drum was sometimes referred to as the heartbeat of Mother Earth.

Family, Community, Language, Culture, and Religion

Remote Mission

Missionaries from Europe began reaching out to the Native population in the seventeenth century. Many people converted to Christianity, and others continued with their traditional spiritual practices. Some followed a combination of both belief systems.

Missionary Settlement

In 1717, the Seminary of St. Sulpice of Paris built a Native village on the shore of Lake of Two Mountains near Oka, Quebec. Later it became the Kanesatake Reserve. The cross was placed on the hill in 1739 as a pilgrimage for the Indigenous peoples. They would visit the church before leaving in the fall to go hunting.

Early Church-Run Schools

Churches set up Christian schools in the early 1800s. Some Indigenous peoples were eager to have their children educated by the missionaries and were happy to send them. Other parents chose to continue to educate children in their traditional ways. Attendance at these schools was voluntary. This image is of a prayer meeting with Roman Catholic clergy in 1870.

Travelling Missionaries
This watercolour by Maria Spilsbury shows a group of Inuit listening to a visiting preacher in Nain, Labrador.

Sweat Lodge
One of the ceremonies that many Aboriginal groups across Canada took part in was the sweat lodge. Sweat lodges were used for purification ceremonies, prayer, and healing. These Tsuu T'ina men were photographed in a sweat lodge on a reserve in Alberta in the early 1900s.

Family, Community, Language, Culture, and Religion

Educating the Children

Aboriginal communities shared the responsibilities of raising and educating their children. Although there were no formal schools or classrooms, children were nonetheless being educated on a daily basis. They were taught proper behaviour and skills by example. Play was also an important part of their education. Children were given toy cooking implements and tools and child-size bows and arrows to play with. Morals were taught through storytelling and children were expected to do chores and help out at a young age. The elders in the community were some of the most important teachers. They passed on the traditions of culture and language to ensure the continuation of their nations.

Sisters
Girls were expected to help take care of their siblings, which prepared them to be mothers themselves.

"They love their children dearly."
– Gabriel Sagard

Mother and Daughter
Indigenous boys learned how to hunt, fish, and fight by observing their elders. Girls learned how to care for children, sew, and cook by observing their mothers and other women. They grew up knowing their roles in the group. This photo shows an Ojibwa woman with her baby in a cradleboard in 1858. Missionaries, such as Gabriel Sagard, observed the close bond between Aboriginal parents and their children. "They love their children dearly," he wrote.

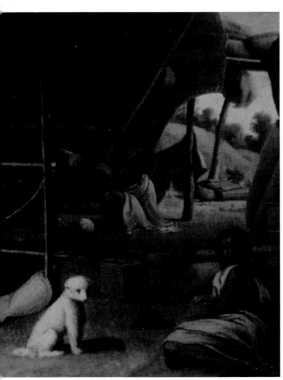

Learning by Watching

Native girls observed their mothers and learned how to light campfires, cook, and do the washing. They would practise their own parenting skills on dolls that were made by their mothers, sewing clothes for them, and using the skills that would translate into adulthood. This nineteenth-century painting shows a Native camp north of Quebec City.

Learning to Weave

Paul Kane's painting shows a Salish woman weaving one of their renowned blankets. She likely used wool from the Salish Wool Dog sitting beside her. Children would learn skills such as weaving by watching their mothers.

Boys and Dogs

Boys bonded with their dogs while doing chores together. Dogs were pets and co-workers for Aboriginal children. They would help children with chores such as hauling wood. Some dogs also helped in hunting. They would help transport the families' belongings by carrying or dragging them to the next camp.

Learning Skills

At home, children began to learn skills such as hunting through playing with weapons that were designed for them. A Kwagiulth man from British Columbia recalls, "Every boy had bows and arrows. My brother made them for me, and we used to go out in canoes bought by my brother from the people that made them." The boys would practise shooting at ducks, hoping to bring one home to their mother.

Educating the Children

Learning and Playing

Traditionally, Aboriginal children were taught by their families and communities and were given responsibilities at a young age. They were expected to help care for younger children, hunt, and fish. Children were taught by the examples of their elders. In this image, the kids are imitating their elders by fishing, setting up their own little camp, and cooking the fish.

Spearfishing

A father and son are spearfishing together in the above photo. Boys would practise sitting perfectly still in the canoe, then shoot arrows or throw a spear at floating weeds to hone their skills. Children began hunting early and each kill was celebrated by their families.

Early Hockey

Aboriginal children played a game similar to hockey or lacrosse on the ice using carved sticks. The first games of this kind observed by Europeans were played by the Mi'kmaq in Nova Scotia in the 1600s.

Children were taught by the examples of their elders.

Young men played games to compete against one another and show off their skills. These young Northern Plains men are playing the game of arrows. The object of the game was to shoot as many arrows as possible into the air before the first one hits the ground. Highly skilled contestants could shoot up to eight arrows in rapid succession before the first one came down. These skills were useful for hunting and in battle.

Storytelling

Isabelle Knockwood, a residential school Survivor from Nova Scotia, recalls, "The elders started their stories by saying, 'Sa'qewey na,' which means, 'This originates in antiquity.' This indicated to the listeners that what they were about to say was passed down to them through their great-grandparents. So some of the legends that I and my brothers and sister heard were at least seven generations old."

Learning through Stories

Trickster characters appear in the myths of many Aboriginal cultures, often as a raven or a coyote that could change shape into a human. Tricksters could be villains or heroes. Sometimes they were used to teach morals or appropriate behaviour to children. Storytelling was also considered entertainment and passed time during cold winter months. Stories included such tales as "Why Porcupine Has Quills" and "The Story of the Great Flood".

Educating the Children   35

The Talking Stick
This elder, Hamasaka, was photographed with a talking stick, in Qagyuhl, British Columbia, around 1914. A talking stick was a symbol of authority. At council meetings, the talking stick could be passed from person to person, indicating who had a right to speak.

Oral Traditions and Elders
The knowledge of elders in Native communities was highly valued. Traditions, stories, and songs were passed down verbally by the elders. These oral traditions served not only to entertain, but also to teach children moral lessons and proper behaviour.

Six Nations Education
This illustration appeared in *A Primer for the Use of the Mohawk Children*, which was published in 1786. Thayendanegea, also known as Joseph Brant, an important Aboriginal leader following the American Revolution, and his followers believed that it was important for Six Nations children to receive a European education, but not at the expense of their Iroquoian heritage.

Life Before the Schools

LESSON XXXIV

1. Look! the cars are coming.
Sâtsit! istsi-enakâs epoxapoyaw.

2. They come very fast.
Ixka-ekkami-poxapoyaw.

3. They come from Winnipeg.
Mikutsitartay omortsipoxapoyaw.

4. The cars are full of people.
Matapix itortoyitsiyaw enakâsix.

5. Let us go to the depot.
Konnê-ctâpoôp istsi-enakâs-api-oyis.

Church-Based Schools

The *Indian Act* of 1876 placed restrictions on the education of Aboriginal children. Many children were voluntarily sent to church-run schools, where they were instructed in the Christian faith. Above is a page from *First Reader in the English and Blackfoot Languages* from 1886.

Early Residential Schools

Before the Canadian government developed their plans to assimilate Aboriginal children through the education system, churches began establishing residential schools in the 1840s. This photo shows Reverend Ferrier taking boys to school at Portage la Prairie, Manitoba, in 1904.

The *Indian Act* of 1876 placed restrictions on the education of Aboriginal children.

Shoal Lake School

Shoal Lake school, the precursor of Cecilia Jeffrey school near Kenora, Ontario, opened at the turn of the twentieth century on terms acceptable to Chief Red Sky and his council. The chief agreed to more formal education, as long as his community's traditions and culture were taught and respected. There would also be no punishment for children who did not attend.

CHAPTER 2
CONFLICT ARISING FROM CONTACT

Crown and Aboriginal Sovereignties

In 1857, the *Act to Encourage the Gradual Civilization of Indian Tribes* allowed Aboriginals in Canada to become full British subjects, as long as they were willing to give up their lands, languages, cultures, and existing rights. The British Crown — and the local government acting in the name of the Crown — believed that its way of life, culture, and values were superior to those of the First Nations peoples and began seeking greater control over them through treaties. The intent was to assert ownership and control by the Canadian government and the Crown over Native land, resources, and people. Realizing that the Aboriginal population could be a serious threat if they got together and fought back, the government offered promises of housing, healthcare, education, and hunting territories. Once treaties were signed, however, the Crown and the government often neglected to make good on their promises and treaty commitments.

Pushing Out the Mi'kmaq
A nineteenth-century painting shows a Mi'kmaq family on the East Coast cooking a lobster. Although life appears idyllic, the Mi'kmaq were being forced off their land. The most fertile and resource-heavy lands by the water were steadily taken over by settlers.

The Treaty Process

The Canadian government negotiated treaties and committed to making payments to First Nations peoples without knowing how many Aboriginal people there were or how much the payments would cost. After sending in census takers, as shown on the left, to determine the Indigenous population, the government was dismayed to find out how large the population actually was. That realization was also important in the event of resistance. The government had to assess the strength of their military compared to the potential strength of the Native population. The government wanted to assert its strength and gain control over the land without sparking an uprising.

> " Canada asserted control over Aboriginal land. In some locations, Canada negotiated Treaties with First Nations; in others, the land was simply occupied or seized. The negotiation of Treaties, while seemingly honourable and legal, was often marked by fraud and coercion. "

Truth and Reconciliation
Commission of Canada
Volume One: Summary, p.1

Louis Riel

Louis Riel was a well-educated Metis man. He became a prominent political leader when the federal government took over control of western Canadian land from the Hudson's Bay Company without consulting the residents. Riel led the formation of a provisional government in the Red River area around Winnipeg. He then negotiated terms with the federal government for the establishment of the province of Manitoba in 1870. In 1885, Metis residents of what became Saskatchewan were in a conflict over land and their rights with the federal government. With Riel, this Metis group offered armed resistance to the federal authorities to try to retain control over their own land. The conflict was termed the North-West Rebellion of 1885.

Crowfoot and His Family

Crowfoot, or Isapo-muxika, was a leader of the Siksika people and is pictured in the centre of this photo in 1884. He was part of negotiations for what became Treaty Seven. Although he was an experienced warrior, he refused to join the North-West Rebellion. Treaty Seven forced Aboriginal peoples to give up their traditional territories and live on a reserve in what is now the province of Alberta.

Crown and Aboriginal Sovereignties

Acquiring Resources

Scorched Earth, Clear-Cut Logging on Native Sovereign Land. Shaman Coming to Fix is the title of this contemporary painting by artist Lawrence Paul Yuxweluptun. It refers to the land claim process used by the federal government.

Setting Aside Reserves

This image shows St. Regis Reserve (now known as the Akwesasne Reserve) in the early nineteenth century. Located near Cornwall, Ontario, it was one of the earliest Iroquoian reserves to be established. When First Nations peoples agreed to move onto reserves and sign treaties, they were told that the treaty land would provide them with enough resources to continue hunting and gathering their food. Often this wasn't the case. Also, the other benefits that were promised, such as housing and health care, were either not provided or were much less than promised.

Lorette

Lorette, Quebec, was established for refugee Christian Huron people and is one of the country's oldest reserve settlements. This watercolour by Henry William Barnard depicts the village in 1838.

Conflict Arising from Contact

Thayendanegea

Thayendanegea, also know by the English name of Joseph Brant, is honoured in this painting by William Berczy. Thayendanegea was a Mohawk leader and one of Britain's most important Loyalist allies in upper New York during the American Revolution. He played a vital role in the creation of the Six Nations reserve on the Grand River in Ontario. The reserve, originally six miles wide on both sides of the river, was granted by British colonial authorities to their Native allies who opted to move to British territory after the Revolution.

Blackfoot Reserve

This image shows Jim Abikoki and his family in front of the fence surrounding the Anglican Mission on the Blackfoot Reserve in Alberta, around 1900.

Crown and Aboriginal Sovereignties

Assimilation: A Government Policy

Divide and Conquer
Prime Minister John A. Macdonald on his policy of sending Aboriginal children to residential schools: "When the school is on the reserve, the child lives with his parents who are savages; he is surrounded by savages, and though he may learn to read and write, his habits and training and mode of thought are Indian. He is simply a savage who can read and write."

From 1867, the Canadian government saw relations with Aboriginal peoples as the "Indian problem." Political leaders and bureaucrats decided on a policy of assimilation. The goal was to eliminate all elements of Native culture so that Aboriginals behaved the same as non-Native Canadians. Officials focused on Aboriginal children. They decided that by removing the children completely from the influence of their families and communities, they could "kill the Indian" while educating them. There was also the belief that once trained, Aboriginal youth would enter the workforce and provide a much needed source of labour. This would limit the need for immigrant labour. The government partnered with Christian missionaries to establish residential schools that encouraged the children to convert to Christianity. The schools received some federal funding, but were meant to be mostly self-sufficient.

A British Education
Lawrence Vankoughnet was the federal Deputy Minister of Indian Affairs from 1874 to 1893. He believed that removing Aboriginal children from their communities was the only way "of advancing the Indian in civilization," as he wrote in a letter to Prime Minister Macdonald. Despite treaty promises, the government did not provide schools on most reserves.

The *Gradual Civilization Act*
The government enacted the *Gradual Civilization Act* in 1857. Aboriginal and Metis men over twenty-one who wished to become citizens with the same rights as all other Canadians were obliged to read, write, and speak either English or French. They were also required to choose a surname, which had to be approved by the government. In doing so, they became British subjects and lost all legal rights and claims to any land. The purpose of this "enfranchisement" was to completely assimilate them and "take the Indian out" of them. The photos to the left show a First Nations man before assimilation and after (small inset).

THE OLD FLAG.
THE OLD POLICY,
THE OLD LEADER.

Playing Dress-Up
Hayter Reed, pictured here with his son at a costume ball in Ottawa in 1896, was Canada's Deputy Minister of Indian Affairs after Vankoughnet. Reed did not believe that the federal government had any responsibility for the education of Metis children.

Assimilation: Not a Single Indian Not Absorbed
Duncan Campbell Scott, the federal Deputy Minister of Indian Affairs from 1913 to 1932, was focused on the day when "there is not a single Indian in Canada who has not been absorbed into the body politic." He and his fellow officials understood that the aggressive removal of Aboriginal children would have an impact not only on them and their families, but on future generations. Scott was also a writer and poet and was considered to be a leading Canadian literary figure.

Assimilation: A Government Policy

Assimilation Policy and Practice

Aboriginal peoples were expected to give up everything relating to their heritage in exchange for full British citizenship. If they learned to read and signed a pledge to "live as a white," they could vote, serve on juries, and own property — but they would lose all Aboriginal rights. The Canadian government's *Indian Act* allowed for protection of First Nations land — but the government held the title and controlled it. Laws were put into place to severely restrict the rights of First Nations peoples. For example, it became illegal for them to buy or consume alcohol without renouncing their Aboriginal status.

> **" The intent of the government's policy, which was firmly established in legislation at the time that the Treaties had been negotiated, was to assimilate Aboriginal people into broader Canadian society. At the end of this process, Aboriginal people were expected to have ceased to exist as a distinct people with their own governments, cultures, and identities. "**
>
> Truth and Reconciliation Commission of Canada
> Volume One: Summary, p.57

NOTICE is hereby given th
selling or giving, directly
to Indians, any INTOXICA

INTOXICATING F

in the form of patent or
medicines, cordials or perf
on or off their Reserves, w
cuted with the utmost ri
law, being liable to a fine o

$300.0

and to SIX MONTHS impr
R. A.

Department of Mines and Resources,
Indian Affairs Branch,
Ottawa

I.A. 1037
R. 3187

Controlling Freedoms

The *Indian Act* gave the federal government the right to create regulations that would govern Aboriginal peoples and exert control over them. In this case, the government determined that alcohol could not be sold to Aboriginals. Someone who wanted the right to drink alcohol legally had to renounce their status as an Aboriginal person.

y person
directly,
, or any

D

prietary
s, either
e prose-
of the

ment.
EY,

of Indian Affairs.

NOTICE

THIS CERTIFICATE IS NOT TRANSFERABLE AND SHOULD BE CAREFULLY PRESERVED AS DUPLICATE CANNOT BE ISSUED UNLESS ABSOLUTE PROOF OF LOSS IS FURNISHED.

DEPARTMENT OF CITIZENSHIP AND IMMIGRATION INDIAN AFFAIRS BRANCH OTTAWA CANADA

CANADA

CERTIFICATE OF ENFRANCHISEMENT

Enfranchisement

Indigenous people were coerced into giving up their status and given certificates of enfranchisement. With these papers, they could vote in federal elections, sue the government, and obtain rights that were otherwise denied to them by the *Indian Act*.

Pass System

Once Aboriginal families relocated to reserves, their movements were severely restricted. If they needed to leave the reserve for any reason, they had to have the written permission of a government employee called an "Indian agent."

Amendment to the Indian Act

The 1884 *Amendment to the Indian Act* gave the Canadian government the authority to create Indian residential schools. The government funded and operated the schools with the cooperation of churches. The purpose of educating Aboriginal children in residential schools was to remove them from the influence of their families.

Assimilation Policy and Practice

Cutting Cultural Ties

In the 1880s, assimilation became more and more widespread. Aboriginal women who married non-Aboriginal men were forced to give up not only their own status, but the status of their children. One of the most significant bans placed on Aboriginal peoples by the Amendment to the *Indian Act* in 1884 was the ban on ceremonies such as Sun Dances and potlatches. First Nations peoples were no longer permitted to perform ceremonies that had been handed down for generations and the traditional costumes and items used in the celebrations were seized from them and sold. Banning these events was another step towards eliminating Aboriginal culture and stopping its transmission to future generations.

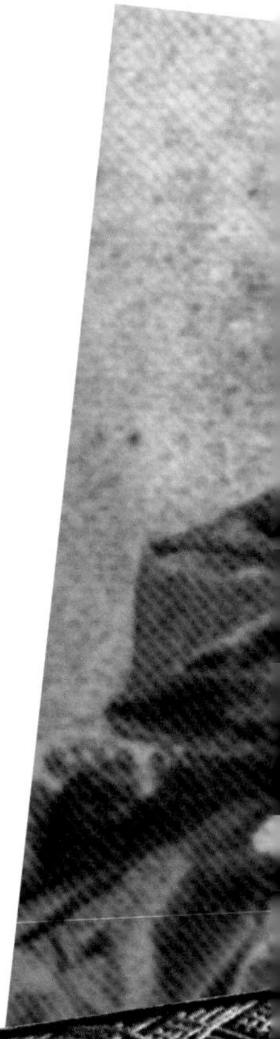

Potlatch Prohibition

Chief Clelaman, from Bella Coola, BC, celebrated a potlatch in 1892, despite the government ban. This image shows an inscription celebrating his potlatch over the doorway of his house. According to the *Indian Act*: "Every Indian or other person who engages in or assists in celebrating the Indian festival known as the 'Potlatch' or the Indian dance known as the 'Tamanawas' is guilty of a misdemeanor, and shall be liable to imprisonment for a term not more than six nor less than two months in a jail or other place of confinement."

Illegal Production

The *Amendment to the Indian Act* made it illegal for Indigenous people to sell or produce goods, such as the birchbark box shown above, without the permission of the Indian agent. This caused great hardship for people who relied on trading to feed and clothe their families.

Racism

Unions between Aboriginal and non-Aboriginal people — and the Metis children they produced — were often shunned by European and Indigenous communities alike. Amelia Douglas, pictured here, was a Metis woman who was married to James Douglas, the governor of Vancouver Island from 1851 to 1864. She faced discrimination with grace and always presented herself as the quintessential Victorian lady.

> " Although, in most of their official pronouncements, government and church officials took the position that Aboriginal people could be civilized, it is clear that many believed that Aboriginal culture was inherently inferior. "
>
> Truth and Reconciliation
> Commission of Canada
> Volume One: Summary, p.4

Seizure of Cultural Artifacts

This painting portrays Pacific Coast First Nations peoples dressed in potlatch attire, around 1896. The Canadian government considered the potlatch ceremony to be barbaric. Officials believed that Aboriginal peoples could not possibly better themselves unless potlatches were banned. After it outlawed the ceremonies, the government seized the regalia of many West Coast peoples and sold it to Canadian and American museums.

Cutting Cultural Ties

CHAPTER 3

THE CHILDREN ARE TAKEN

Forced Removal

Residential schools were established in 1878. They were modelled after reformatories and industrial schools established in Britain as penal institutions for children of the urban poor. The Canadian government also drew inspiration from institutions set up in the United States. The government established partnerships with a number of churches, including the Roman Catholic church, the Anglican Church, and what became the United Church. The churches operated the schools under agreements with the government, which paid for the system. In 1920, the government made attendance at the schools compulsory for Aboriginal children. Indian agents began visiting Aboriginal families and taking the children. If parents refused, they were punished harshly. The family allowance from the Canadian government was withheld and in some cases parents were arrested and spent time in jail. The *Indian Act* did not initially include Inuit peoples. It wasn't until 1939 that the government took responsibility for educating Inuit children, too.

Truant Officers and Enforcement

The Royal Canadian Mounted Police was the police force with jurisdiction regarding Aboriginal peoples. The RCMP actively enforced the *Indian Act* and the pass system that was put in place to limit people's movements outside reserve lands. The RCMP enforced the government ban on alcohol and ceremonial dances. They also acted as truant officers. Their job was not only to ensure that children were taken away to school, but also that they stayed at school. Officers would pursue runaways and return them to school.

Forcible Removal

In 1920, the *Indian Act* was changed to make attendance at residential schools mandatory for Aboriginal children between the ages of seven and fifteen. Children as young as six were rounded up by Indian agents or the RCMP and taken from their families, by force if necessary. Churches got court injunctions, which threatened parents with jail if they didn't send their children to the schools.

Family Allowance Threatened
Residential school Survivor Lillian Elias says, "I don't remember why they had to send me to school until later on in the years, after I had been there for three or four years, I found out that the reason they had to put me in there was because they were going to lose my Family Allowance, or all the children's Family Allowance if one of the children didn't go to school. So my parents thought I was the bravest one to go to school. They thought I could cope with the things that were going on."

" It can start with a knock on the door one morning. It is the local Indian agent, or the parish priest, or, perhaps, a Mounted Police officer. The bus for residential school leaves that morning. It is a day the parents have long been dreading. Even if the children have been warned in advance, the morning's events are still a shock. The officials have arrived and the children must go.

For tens of thousands of Aboriginal children for over a century, this was the beginning of their residential schooling. They were torn from their parents, who often surrendered them only under threat of prosecution. "

Truth and Reconciliation
Commission of Canada
Volume One: Summary, p.41

Being Taken from Home
Children were transported from their homes to residential schools by trucks, boats, and airplanes.

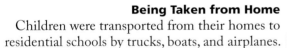

Homesick
Marjorie Flowers flew from Makkovik to North West River in Labrador to attend Lake Melville High School. "I didn't realize how hard it would be until I got on the plane," she says. "Then I realized I was leaving my parents. So I cried the whole way. By the time I got to school at North West River my eyes were almost swollen shut. I was just sad. So I basically cried the whole first week, for sure."

Forced Removal

Separation

Separation was equally hard on the children and their parents. Some parents felt that they were giving their children the chance at a better life and willingly allowed them to leave. Others tried to hide their children from the officials who arrived to take them. Many parents suffered guilt and turned to alcohol to deal with the stress and pain.

On the Way to School
Aboriginal children shown on their way to Hay River School in the Northwest Territories.

School Application
Some parents applied for admission to residential schools because they felt that their children would be better off at school where they could gain an education and learn a trade that would help them fit into the new society. Often, parents couldn't afford to feed their children and they believed that the school could afford to take better care of them.

"Suddenly I began to remember the old people's stories about black robes and faces pale as death."

Leaving Family
Native children are pictured with their parents outside a schoolhouse in the Northwest Territories.

Scared at School
Isabelle Knockwood, far left, recalls arriving at the Indian Residential School at Shubenacadie, Nova Scotia: "At the top of the steps the heavy wooden doors with glass panels stood ajar and, just as we reached the top, a priest and nun came out. The priest extended a pale hand. From where I was standing, all I could see was the hand and the black robes. My father took the hand and shook it. My mother smiled stiffly and I began to sense something wrong. My mouth filled up with spit and I felt as if I might throw up. Suddenly I began to remember the old people's stories about black robes and faces pale as death."

Saying Goodbye
Students at Fort Simpson Residential School in the Northwest Territories hold up letters spelling "goodbye" in 1922.

Letters Home

Like most children, Marjorie Flowers was overwhelmed by homesickness. She attended Lake Melville High School in Labrador from grades nine to eleven. "I remember being very homesick. I didn't want to be in school there. I wanted to be home."

Marjorie Flowers:

"I didn't want to go by the rules but yet I knew if I didn't then I would be in trouble. So I would write these letters home to my parents and make little teardrops. I wanted them to see how sad I was and I thought if I did that, or if I didn't do well in school then maybe they would let me come home."

Aboriginal Schoolboy

Theodore Fontaine, pictured here at age ten, went to Fort Alexander Indian Residential School in Manitoba for ten years, beginning when he was seven.

Theodore Fontaine:

"Me on the steps of Fort Alexander Indian Residential School, Manitoba, in 1950 (my third year there). My mother had this image made into a Christmas greeting card that year. She must have seen family photos on Christmas cards in the homes of the white ladies she worked for."

Students and Parents
Being taken from their parents was devastating for Aboriginal children and heartbreaking for their parents.

Hard Times Ahead
A former residential school student remembers: "I started to whimper, not understanding why but sensing that something awful was about to happen to me. Mom consoled me and held on tightly to my hand. Hers felt warm, protective, and soft in spite of the roughness caused by years of constant hard work. Her glance was gentle and loving and her lovely brown eyes were beginning to tear."

Parent Visit
Although some parents could visit their children's residential schools, often Aboriginal students didn't see their parents for months or even years. Some children were angry at being left and took it out on their parents, refusing to interact with them when they visited or when they returned home.

> " Older brothers were separated from younger brothers, older sisters were separated from younger sisters, and brothers and sisters were separated from each other. "

Truth and Reconciliation
Commission of Canada
Volume One: Summary, p.44

CHAPTER 4
LIFE AT RESIDENTIAL SCHOOL

Shock

The shock was immediate for children taken away to school. They were suddenly surrounded by white faces speaking a foreign language that they often didn't understand. Once at the schools, their hair was cut, they were stripped of their own clothes, and forced to wear uniform-like clothing that was completely foreign to their experience. They were fed a diet of unfamiliar food. Speaking their own language was strictly forbidden and harshly punished. Boys and girls were separated from each other, which meant that often brothers and sisters rarely saw each other.

Hopelessness
Fifteen-year-old Ziewe is pictured here shortly after being delivered to residential school. Her look in this photo reflects the hopelessness that many students felt.

Compulsory Haircuts
Upon entering the school, children had their hair cut, often for the first time. Since hair was culturally important, the authorities decided that cutting the hair would also help sever ties to the students' heritage.

Campbell Papequash:

> "And after I was taken there they took off my clothes and then they deloused me. I didn't know what was happening but I learned about it later, that they were delousing me; 'the dirty, no-good-for-nothing savages, lousy.' And then they cut off my beautiful hair. You know and my hair, my hair represents such a spiritual significance of my life and my spirit. And they did not know, you know, what they were doing to me. You know and I cried and I see them throw my hair into a garbage can, my long, beautiful braids. And then after they deloused me then I was thrown into the shower, you know, to go wash all that kerosene off my body and off my head. And I was shaved, bald-headed."

Losing Identity
This image of a First Nations girl having her braids cut off comes from the picture book *Fatty Legs* by Christy Jordan-Fenton and Margaret Pokiak-Fenton.

Isabelle Knockwood
Isabelle Knockwood, pictured here, and her sister Rosie were students at the Indian Residential School in Shubenacadie, Nova Scotia, from 1936 to 1947. She was only five years old when she was put in school.

Shirley Williams
"When I saw [the school] it was grey. A brick building when it rains is dark and grey, you know. It's an ugly day but the feeling was . . . of ugliness. [T]he gate opened and the bus went in, and I think when the gate closed . . . something happened to me, something locked, it is like my heart locked, because it could hear that [clink of gates]." Shirley attended St. Joseph's Girls School in Spanish, Ontario, from the age of ten.

Isabelle Knockwood:
"Our home clothes were stripped off and we were put in the tub. When we got out we were given new clothes with wide black and white vertical stripes. Much later I discovered that this was almost identical to the prison garb of the time. We were also given numbers. I was 58 and Rosie was 57."

Assimilation

As Peter Irniq recalls, the school wasted no time trying to erase years of traditional upbringing. "We had overnight become white men and white women, little children. We were beginning to be taught to become like a European at this particular school."

New Clothing

Peter Irniq attended Sir Joseph Bernier Federal Day School in Chesterfield Inlet, in what is now Nunavut. "There they took our clothes, our traditional clothing. I was wearing sealskin boots. They took all of our traditional clothing and for the first time I saw and wore shoes. For the first time I saw a pair of jeans. For the first time I saw a short-sleeved shirt and that's what we were wearing."

> " Taken from their homes, stripped of their belongings, and separated from their siblings, residential school children lived in a world dominated by fear, loneliness, and lack of affection. "

Truth and Reconciliation
Commission of Canada
Volume One: Summary, p.45

Before and After

This telling pair of images conveys clearly the objective of the residential schools. The two photos show Thomas Moore. On the left, he is dressed in his traditional clothing before going to the Regina Indian Industrial School in 1891. On the right is Thomas Moore in a school outfit. The pair of images was intended to show that the goal of assimilating children into European society was being successfully achieved.

Losing Their Language
In the classroom, only English or French could be spoken. Students were beaten or even had needles stuck through their tongues if they were caught speaking to each other in their own language.

Dormitories
Isabelle Knockwood recalls, "The dormitories were kept spotless, with polished hardwood floors, which were always cold. I was never warm at school. There were never enough blankets. Sometimes at night I would get up and put on my stockings. Sometimes I kept my stockings on when I went to bed. I missed my nice warm bed at home. Rosie and I had always slept together. It was always warm in our house."

Separating Brothers and Sisters
Boys and girls were kept strictly separate. In many cases, brothers and sisters didn't see or speak to each other at all.

Starvation

After being raised on a diet of freshly caught fish, fresh and dried meat, berries, and bannock, children were expected to eat porridge made of cracked wheat, dried beans, and processed meat, which had very little nutritional value. Children were never fed enough to feel full. Staff sometimes used the funds allocated for students' food to buy themselves steak and potatoes, while the children were forced to eat mush and rancid meat. Children were forced to work in fields, gardens, and barns to produce fresh vegetables and milk that were not used to feed the children, but sold instead. The objective was to reduce costs, with no concern for student nutrition or health.

Mealtime

There was not enough food and children never felt full. Porridge was a staple of the residential school diet. Made from cracked wheat, it often became lumpy and slimy. George Manuel, a student at the Kamloops School, remembers, "Hunger is both the first and the last thing I can remember about that school . . . Every Indian student smelled of hunger." This photo was taken at the Qu'Appelle Industrial School, Saskatchewan.

> " The federal government knowingly chose not to provide schools with enough money to ensure that kitchens and dining rooms were properly equipped, that cooks were properly trained, and, most significantly, that food was purchased in sufficient quantity and quality for growing children. It was a decision that left thousands of Aboriginal children vulnerable to disease. "

Truth and
Reconciliation
Commission of Canada
Volume One: Summary, p.92

Stealing Food

Hungry children took potatoes that they were harvesting and roasted them in the fire. Frederick Loft attended the Mohawk Institute in Brantford, Ontario. "I recall the times when working in the fields, I was actually too hungry to be able to walk, let alone work."

Starvation

Government officials were aware of the inadequate food at residential schools. Although expected to serve the teachers healthy dinners, the students were left with meals consisting of rancid food or mush that they were forced to consume or starve. This letter was written September 16, 1953, to P. E. Moore, Medical Director of Indian Affairs. "Children at the Brandon Indian Industrial School are not being fed properly to the extent that they are garbaging around in the barns for food that should only be fed to the barn occupants."

Hunger

The children often had the same meals daily. Porridge with skim milk was breakfast. The midday meal was mush or a sort of stew with a slice of bread with no butter. Supper was the same mush and some sort of vegetable. For children who were used to a healthy diet, the change to processed meats, cheese, and cooked vegetables was drastic.

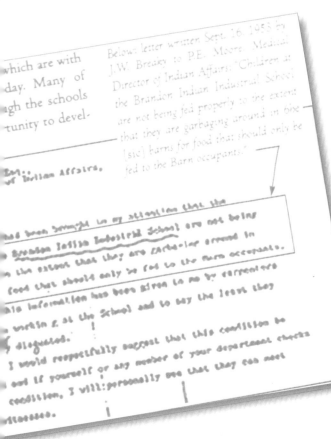

which are with day. Many of gh the schools tunity to devel-

Below: letter written Sept. 16, 1953 by J.W. Breaky to P.E. Moore, Medical Director of Indian Affairs: "Children at the Brandon Indian Industrial School are not being fed properly to the extent that they are garbaging around in [the] [sic] barns for food that should only be fed to the Barn occupants."

"**Hunger is both the first and the last thing I can remember about that school . . . Every Indian student smelled of hunger.**"

Education in English and French

A typical day for children at residential school was broken into two parts. Only two to four hours were spent in class. The rest of the day was spent working, to reduce the need to spend money on school facilities and staff. Students worked at farming, carpentry, and domestic chores. The daily routine was strictly regimented, a difficult adjustment for many.

The Kamloops, BC, School Day
The boys typically got up at 5:30 a.m. to do barn chores, such as milking and feeding the animals. The girls rose at 6:00 a.m. and got dressed and ready for the day. Three hundred sixty-five days a year the children attended morning Mass, followed by breakfast and morning chores. The school day began with an hour of religious studies, followed by two hours of regular classes like math and reading. The rest of the day was filled with chores. Girls would sew, do laundry, cook, or clean. The boys worked outside gardening, farming, or learning carpentry. The rest of the day was filled with study time, dinner, cleaning, and some recreation time before prayers and bedtime.

Classroom Time
Morning classes would typically take only a couple of hours during the day. With so little classroom time, few students progressed past the first few grade levels.

> " ... Most of the residential schools operated on what was referred to as the 'half-day system.' Under this system — which amounted to institutionalized child labour — students were in class for half the day and in what was supposed to be vocational training for the other half. Often, as many students, teachers, and inspectors observed, the time allocated for vocational training was actually spent in highly repetitive labour that provided little in the way of training. Rather, it served to maintain the school operations. As educational institutions, the residential schools were failures, and regularly judged as such. "

Truth and Reconciliation
Commission of Canada
Volume One: Summary, p.74

Road to Learning
Shirley Williams attended St. Joseph's Indian Residential School in Fort William, Ontario (now Thunder Bay). "In school we learned many different subjects such as English, science, math, writing, geography, history, and home economics. The home economics consisted of knitting, cooking, and sewing."

The Sewing Room
At Lejac Indian Residential School in Fraser Lake, BC, the girls spent most of the afternoon in the sewing room. In one year they made 293 dresses, 191 aprons, 296 pairs of underwear, 301 undershirts, and 600 pairs of socks.

> " Of her experiences at the Baptist school in Whitehorse and the Anglican school in Carcross, Rose Dorothy Charlie said, 'They took my language. They took it right out of my mouth. I never spoke it again.' "

Truth and Reconciliation
Commission of Canada
Volume One: Summary, p.86

Education in English and French

Harvesting

Theodore Fontaine recalls, "In my third or fourth year, I was one of the boys to help in the fall harvest. The boys in grades four to eight were pulled out of classes for this."

Kitchen Duties

Students were required to work in school kitchens making bread, churning butter, cooking, and cleaning.

Mending Clothes

Isabelle Knockwood shared, "Everyone I interviewed liked the sewing Sisters, Clita and Rita, because they never yelled or scolded, but taught sewing in a calm and patient way. Both were gentle souls and allowed us to talk and laugh as long as we were reasonably quiet."

> **Inspectors viewed the continued use of Aboriginal languages by the students as a sign of failure.**
>
> Truth and Reconciliation
> Commission of Canada
> Volume One: Summary, p.84

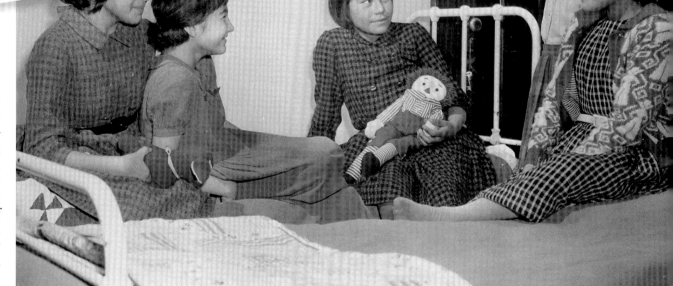

Recreation

If students managed to finish their chores, they were given recreation time to socialize and play with the other students. This staged, propaganda-style photo shows a group of girls at Shingwauk Indian Residential School in Sault Ste. Marie, Ontario.

> **The churches placed a greater priority on religious commitment than on teaching ability. Because the pay was so low, many of the teachers lacked any qualification to teach.**
>
> Truth and Reconciliation
> Commission of Canada
> Volume One: Summary, p.76

Education in English and French

> " . . . These children were sent to what were, in most cases, badly constructed, poorly maintained, overcrowded, unsanitary fire traps. Many children were fed a substandard diet and given a substandard education, and worked too hard. For far too long, they died in tragically high numbers. Discipline was harsh and unregulated; abuse was rife and unreported. It was, at best, institutionalized child neglect. "

Truth and
Reconciliation
Commission of Canada
Volume One: Summary, p.46–7

Boys' Dormitory
"We had a very large dormitory where they had about forty beds, or maybe a little bit more. The beds were all lined up. I was used to a 14-by-12 tent," recalls Peter Irniq.

Prayer
Since the residential schools were run by the churches, there was a lot of emphasis placed on prayer. Children were expected to pray first thing in the morning and then attend Mass and religious studies. They had to pray before bedtime every night, as well. This photo shows children kneeling in prayer on their beds.

Morning Mass
These children and many others were required to attend morning Mass every day of the year.

Bedtime
Children pictured on the left are getting ready for bed by brushing their teeth and getting washed up at a school in Aklavik, Northwest Territories.

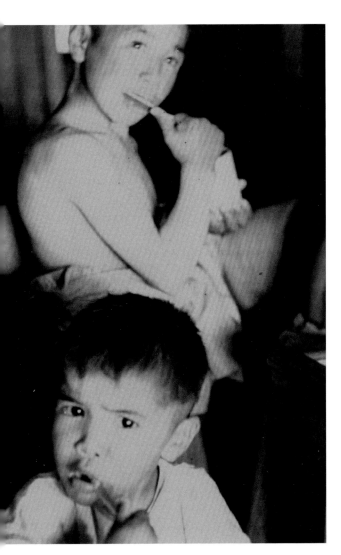

Daily Routine
Janice Acoose of Cowessess, Saskatchewan, recalls the daily routine at her residential school. "Early rise, prayers, shower and dress, meals premised by prayers, school premised by more prayers, rigidly programmed exercise time, catechism instruction and bedtime, which was premised by excruciatingly painful periods of time spent on our knees in prayer circles."

Child Labour

There was a wide range of work that children were expected to do at residential school. Kitchen work could include cooking and baking or cleaning up after meals. Girls worked in the laundry, where they were expected to operate machinery that was often bigger than they were. They also sewed clothing for the students. Boys worked tending to the furnace, raising animals, or caring for crops.

Carrying Wood
Students at All Saints in Lac la Ronge, Saskatchewan, are pictured here in the 1920s. Boys were required to gather wood and do other outdoor tasks, such as farming.

Kitchen Work
Nora Bernard attended the Indian Residential School at Shubenacadie, Nova Scotia. She recalls, "We served a month in the kitchen. I didn't mind going to Mass because it was a break away from the kitchen area."

Harvesting
Harvesting time required extra hands and children were taken out of class for the duration of the harvest season. Every type of vegetable was grown to be sold for profit. Often the only produce held back for the children were potatoes, beans, and turnips. The same crops were grown for the animals.

Kitchen Chores
Rita Joe, a Mi'kmaq poet, spent much of her time at school in Nova Scotia in the kitchen. "For that, you had to get up at four in the morning. We'd bake bread and — oh my God — every second day we'd bake about thirty-five or forty loaves. Holy Lord! And we made soup in a huge pot that was very high and very round. We'd make porridge in the morning, in a big, big porridge pot and we'd boil over two hundred eggs. It was a lot of hard work that we did in the kitchen and the cook could be cruel."

"We'd bake bread and — oh my God — every second day we'd bake about thirty-five or forty loaves."

Workplace Danger
Isabelle Knockwood remembers laundry room accidents. "One cold afternoon, I heard an inhuman-sounding scream. It went through me like cold bellowing wind and chilled me right to the core of my bones. I knew immediately what had happened — one of the girls had got her hand caught in the mangle."

Hard at Work
"Both boys and girls swept, mopped, waxed, and polished all the floors in the school on Saturday morning. The wood floors had to be polished until we could literally see our faces in them," remembers Isabelle Knockwood.

The Inuit Schools

Initially, Inuit were not included in the residential school system. To avoid spending government funds on assimilating this northern Aboriginal population, the government decided that as long as the Inuit made no demands and continued to live off the land, they would be left on their own. In 1939, the Supreme Court of Canada ruled that the Inuit were Indians. This meant the *Indian Act* applied to them as well. In 1951, the first government-regulated school for Inuit opened in Chesterfield Inlet (now part of Nunavut). By 1955, only 15 per cent of Inuit children were in residential schools. By 1964, that number had increased to over 75 per cent.

Bessie Quirt
Bessie Quirt, pictured here in the centre, was a young, single missionary who taught at the first residential school for Inuit children in the Yukon at Shingle Point. She was devoted to her students and was a role model to other women missionaries.

> " The impact of the schools on the Inuit was complex. Some children were sent to schools thousands of kilometres from their homes, and went years without seeing their parents. In other cases, parents who had previously been supporting themselves by following a seasonal cycle of land- and marine-based resource harvesting began settling in communities with hostels so as not to be separated from their children. "

Truth and Reconciliation
Commission of Canada
Volume One: Summary, p.70

Coppermine Tent Hostel
Unlike many schools, students at Coppermine Tent Hostel (in what is now Nunavut) lived in wood-framed field tents.

Learning
Velma MacDonald is pictured here teaching English to First Nations and Inuit children in Inuvik, Northwest Territories, in 1959.

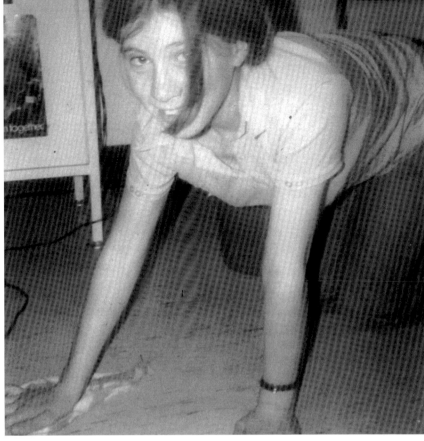

Janitorial Work
As part of her school duties, Marjorie Flowers had to scrub the floor at Lake Melville High School in North West River, Labrador.

Majorie Flowers:
"There was a house parent there who I really became close to. So she became almost like a mother to me. She kind of watched out for me, I think."

Lonely
Peter Irniq, leaning on his hand on the right of the photo, remembers how terrible it was at Sir Joseph Bernier Federal Day School having no contact with his family for nine months.

The Inuit Schools

New Food
Seventeen-year-old Peter Irniq is photographed here at Sir John Franklin High School.

Peter Irniq:

"The one [thing] I used to look forward to during the week, especially at dinner, was eating corned beef. That was something that I got used to fairly quickly and I still like it to this day. The other one that I used to look forward to was Saturday mornings when we would eat corn flakes. So the food to begin with was very horrible. But there were some nice little parts to it when we would have corned beef and corn flakes and things like that."

Happier Times
Peter Irniq, centre front, at the Roman Catholic Mission in Naujaat several years before he attended residential school.

Peter Irniq:

"I remember very happy times when I was a little boy prior to going to the Residential School in Chesterfield Inlet. I lived much like my parents as a very traditional Inuit, the Inuit lifestyle."

Life at Residential School

Hostel Mother
Carolyn Niviaxie's mother was the last hostel mother in the Kuujjuaraapik Federal Hostel. Her job was to look after the students and act as a mother to them when they were away from their own families.

What If?
"If I hadn't been in school I would have been following my family; hunting, camps, everything that they're used to. I grew up in igloos, dog teams, hunger, coldness. That's what I hold on to." Carolyn Niviaxie lived in a hostel in Kuujjuaraapik, Quebec, from the age of seven to sixteen.

Suitcase of Memories
Shirley Flowers brought this suitcase with her when she left for school with her brother. The photo in the suitcase is of Shirley and her brother as they got ready to leave.

Carolyn Niviaxie:

>   "I used to write letters once in a while and my mom used to write me every few months. The letters used to take very long. The only time my mom ever sent me money, it was just five dollars in all that time."

Shirley Flowers:

>   "This suitcase was bought for me when I was going to the dorm to put my stuff in for the winter. All my winter supplies came in that . . . . That's what I took all my winter clothing in, whatever that I needed."

Abuse

In recent years, residential school Survivors spoke up about brutal abuse at the hands of some school staff. Students were subjected to beatings and severe punishments, such as having needles pushed through their tongues for speaking their own language and being forced to wear soiled sheets over their heads for wetting their beds. Physical, mental, and verbal abuse were common, as was sexual abuse. More than 37,000 former students have been compensated for physical and sexual abuse at the schools.

Beatings
Children were subjected to beatings with fists and weapons such as whips or belts.

Neglect
Children had little access to proper medical care. This circa 1905 photo shows students suffering from eye problems without treatment.

“ The failure to develop, implement, and monitor effective discipline sent an unspoken message that there were no real limits on what could be done to Aboriginal children within the walls of a residential school. The door had been opened early to an appalling level of physical and sexual abuse of students, and it remained open throughout the existence of the system. ”

Truth and Reconciliation
Commission of Canada
Volume One: Summary, p.107

Although some priests meant well and showed
kindness toward the children, it was the bad
experiences that stayed with many students and that
fed their fear of anyone in a priest's robe.

Alice Blondin:

"A nun was sponge bathing me and she
proceeded to go a little too far with
her sponge bathing. So I pushed her
hand away. She held my legs apart
while she strapped the inside of my
thighs. I never stopped her again."

Alice Blondin
Alice attended Breynat Hall Residential School in Fort
Smith, Northwest Territories. She is pictured here in grade
eight in the front row on the left.

Martha Joseph spent twelve years
at the Port Alberni Residential
School in BC:

"On one occasion, my hand
was severely burned — by a
staff member who held my hand
down on a hot stove - and
I received this punishment
because I had stolen some
food from the kitchen. I
stole the food because my
little sister, Edna, had
been crying. Edna was crying
because she was so hungry."

Scared
Theodore Fontaine attended Fort
Alexander Residential School in Manitoba.
Below, he describes the above photo.

Theodore Fontaine:

"My classmates and me in about
1949. I'm the little guy at the
front in the solid sweater. At the
far left is my cousin Marcel, who
was enlisted to take me from my
parents on my first day of school.
The principal, Father R., wears the
black robe and cross that made him
look so scary to me that day."

Abuse 73

Terror
Some of the worst instances of abuse came when students dared to speak their own language.

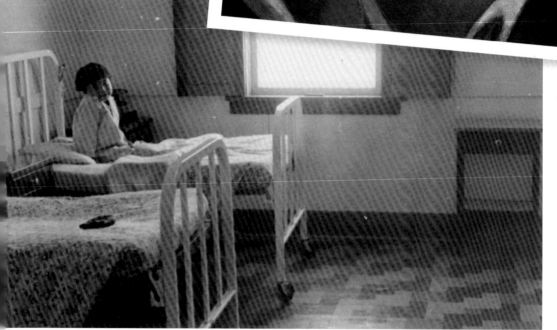

Bedwetting
Bedwetting was punished harshly. Children were forced to wear soiled sheets over their heads and beaten for behaviour that would likely have been resolved with kindness instead of cruelty at home.

Nora Bernard:
"My brother had a problem of bedwetting. They forced him to put on a girl's dress and parade in the refectory in front of all the children and me and my sisters had to sit there and watch his humiliation. I don't know why I didn't run away."

Punished
Theodore, on the left, took up smoking like many of the boys. He was found out by a priest with a strong sense of smell.

Theodore Fontaine:
"Suddenly, he swung his right arm back, and with a quick, deliberate whirling motion, his clenched fist cracked me across my face, clipping my nose . . . I tumbled backward and down into a heap on the concrete floor, blood gushing down my nose . . . The pain felt like I had run into an oak baseball bat."

The Pointer

A thick wooden stick called a pointer was a favourite weapon. Nancy Marble, a student at Shubenacadie, was hit so hard and often that she lost her hearing.

```
Betsey Paul:
    "How many times did I get hit over
    the head with that pointer? That was
    Skite'kmuj's class where she hit me so
    hard she even broke the pointer."
```

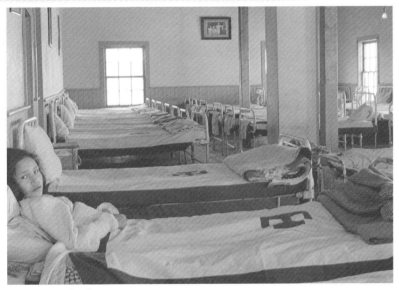

Illness and Abuse

Betsey Paul remembers a girl named Dorothy Doucette who was punished for being ill. "She was so sick, she used to puke right in her plate and Wikew used to beat her in the mouth with a spoon and stuff the food mixed with vomit right back in her mouth again." "Wikew" is Mi'kmaq for "fatty."

Dental Care

Author, community minister, human rights consultant, and field secretary for The International Tribunal into Crimes of Church and State Kevin Annett spoke about the lack of proper dental care for students. "The local dentists were given free Novocaine by the government for the Native kids, but the traditional practice after the war years was for them to hoard the Novocaine for their practice in Port Alberni and just work on the Indians without painkillers. Everyone in the school knew about this and condoned it, from the principal on down."

Some Good Memories

Not all students remember their days at residential school as a negative experience. Some former students recall the friendships they formed and the recreational activities they enjoyed. Some students built on the education they received at school and continued their studies and began successful careers.

Kate Gillespie
Kate Gillespie was appointed principal of the File Hills Residential School, Saskatchewan, in 1901. Until 1904, she donated a third of her income back to the school.

Outdoor Games
Isabelle Knockwood remembers outdoor fun. "When the playgrounds became dry enough, the skipping season began for both girls and boys. Other spring and summer games were basketball, marbles, and of course, hopscotch."

In the Playground
Taking advantage of nice weather, the children played games together outside.

Edna Gregoire, a student at Kamloops School in BC, in the 1930s, has some good memories:

> "The food was nice, we had home-baked bread, and they would make toast out of it, and they had cereal in the morning with nice fresh milk, because they had milk cows there. So I was happy with the food."

Children at Play
In this Moose Factory, Ontario, school, Cree children are wearing headbands and feathers, imitating wild animals.

> **❝** Other students sought solace in the arts. A number of former residential school students went on to prominent careers in the visual arts, including Alex Janvier, Jackson Beardy, Judith Morgan, and Norval Morrisseau. Some, such as Beardy, were encouraged in their artistic endeavours by sympathetic staff. **❞**

Truth and Reconciliation
Commission of Canada
Volume One: Summary, p.115

The Nicer Sisters Made an Impression
Harriette Battiste attended the Shubenacadie school in the early 1930s.

Harriette Battiste:

> "Not all Sisters were bad. Some of them were really nice. They taught us how to tat lace collars which were stylish in those days, crochet doilies, how to decorate our spreads with Mother Goose characters, and to sew fancy designs on the altar cloth by using the button hole stitch."

Playing Outside
Isabelle Knockwood recalls some winter fun. "Some parents sent skis to their children at Christmas time, but the rest of us had to improvise by making skis out of barrel staves from the old apple barrels dumped behind the kitchen. We rubbed them over the cement floor to make them smooth, then waxed and polished them. Then we'd go flying down over that hill all day long."

Some Good Memories

Sports

Some students participated and excelled in sports while at school. This photo shows La Tuque School's hockey team, the Indiens du Quebec.

Christmas Concert

Students are pictured below performing the nativity at their school Christmas concert.

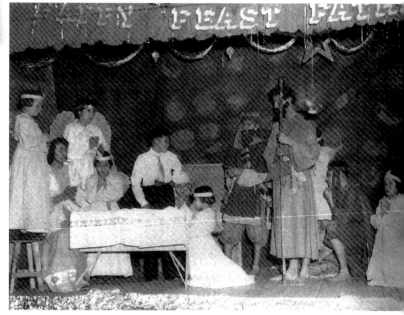

Rita Joe remembers envying the students who got a Christmas present: "Every year, I would ask, 'Is there a parcel there for me?' No, no, never, until that last year I was told, 'Your parcel is there!' I was jumping all over the place; I was so happy. It was from that nun from the laundry. It read 'To Rita from your friend.' I was the happiest fifteen-year-old in the world."

Parent Visits

Qu'Appelle Indian School, Saskatchewan, was one of the few schools that encouraged families to visit. They established a brass band, team sports, and apprenticeships. Not only could parents visit anytime but, against government policy, the school allowed other relatives to visit as well. The main language of instruction was Cree.

Some Devoted Teachers

Judy Jordan taught at Mount Elgin Industrial Institute near London, Ontario. Some teachers believed that their students had value and that their job was an important one. Those were the teachers who made a positive impression.

Graduation

Although many students didn't progress past the first few grades, some went on to graduate high school and continue on to university.

Studying

Adeline Raciette and Emily Bone study on the lawn of the Assiniboia Indian Residential School in Winnipeg, Manitoba.

Cadets

Reverend Lachlan McLean, left, counsels a student soldier in the 1970s. The Cadet programs gave students a chance to learn skills and be part of an important extracurricular activity.

A Wedding

Several teachers attended the weddings of their former students. Some students bonded with their teachers and kept in touch for years.

Some Good Memories

Runaways and Death at School

The death toll at the residential schools has been estimated to be from 3,000 to as high as 6,000. Disease and starvation were common causes of death but many children were killed in fires, committed suicide, or were reportedly beaten to death. Desperate to escape to their homes, children often ran away, despite the hard conditions outside and regardless of the brutal punishment waiting for them when they were inevitably caught. Some died in the attempt.

Death at School

Living in such close quarters caused diseases like tuberculosis and Spanish flu to spread quickly through the staff and students. Death was so common and expected that some schools had cemeteries attached to them.

Prison-like

An anonymous message was attached to this photo of a residential school. "How would you feel if your children were forced to go to a school surrounded by barbed wire fence?"

Running Away from Lejac

On New Year's Day in 1937, four boys ran away from school, trying to get home to their families on the Nautley Reserve in British Columbia. None of them made it. They froze to death within half a mile of their home while crossing a frozen lake. One boy was dressed only in summer clothes with one foot bare. Another was found lying on top of his coat.

> " A January 2015 statistical analysis of the Named Register for the period from 1867 to 2000 identified 2,040 deaths. The same analysis of a combination of the Named and Unnamed registers identified 3,201 reported deaths. The greatest number of these deaths (1,328 on the Named Register and 2,434 on the Named and Unnamed registers) took place prior to 1940. "

Truth and Reconciliation
Commission of Canada
Volume One: Summary, p.93

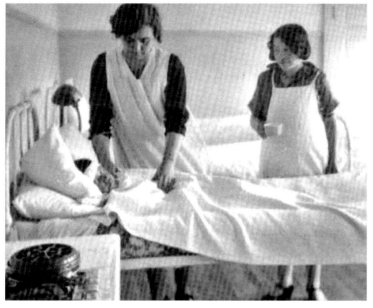

No Fire Escapes

Many schools were built without fire escapes. Instead, poles were provided — outside locked windows. With the windows locked, children couldn't reach the poles and were unable to slide to safety.

Illness at School

According to Dr. P. H. Bryce, the death toll among residential schoolchildren ranged from 15 to 24 per cent — and rose to 42 per cent when the sick children were sent home to die.

The Dungeon

The dungeon was a dark closet where runaway children were locked at Shubenacadie. Their heads were shaved and they were strapped and left in the dungeon. They were taken out at mealtimes where they would eat plain bread and water and then immediately be locked back up.

Residential School Cemetery

The cemetery at the Lac La Ronge Indian School, Saskatchewan, is pictured here around 1920. The youngest child buried there was six years old.

" The buildings were not only fire traps. They were also incubators of disease. Rather than helping combat the tuberculosis crisis in the broader Aboriginal community, the poor condition of the schools served to intensify it. "

Truth and Reconciliation
Commission of Canada
Volume One: Summary, p.97

Funeral for a Student

This funeral vigil was for Jacqueline Basile at Pointe-Bleue Residential School, Quebec, in 1968.

CHAPTER 5

CLOSING THE SCHOOLS

A Failing Grade

It was clear that the residential schools were a failure. Evidence of disease, malnutrition, substandard housing, and abuse mounted. Academically, the schools were not educating their students — most did not progress past grade six. By the early 1940s, the federal government began to re-examine its policy of segregated schools. First Nations peoples demanded more input into the education of their children. The government responded with a gradual replacement of residential schools with a day school model. By 1969, the Department of Indian Affairs had taken complete control of the Aboriginal education system and the church involvement ended. The last residential school closed in 1996.

Industrial School Failure
In 1951, the *Indian Act* was amended and the government changed the schedule that had the children working half days. It was apparent that the industrial school model was a failure. Children were poorly educated and undertrained. The original plan to assimilate graduates into the "white man's world" was misconceived. The harsh reality was that Aboriginal people were the target of discrimination by non-Aboriginal employers. Most young people returned to their reserves — where they no longer fit in.

Delegates
Dave Crowchild, left, and Teddy Yellowfly are pictured here at White River Railway Station in Sudbury, Ontario, en route to a Joint Committee Indian Affairs meeting in Ottawa in 1947.

"Go ahead, change the Indian Act, but Remember I have the last word!!"

Changing the Indian Act
"Go ahead, change the *Indian Act*, but remember I have the last word!!" This Everett Soop cartoon appeared in the *Kainai News* on January 21, 1969. It shows Native men negotiating with Indian Affairs Minister Jean Chrétien. In 1951, major changes were made to the *Indian Act*, removing the ban on Aboriginal ceremonies and traditional practices. In 1961, further changes were made allowing Aboriginal people to keep their status. In spite of these changes, as the cartoon points out, power stayed with the federal government.

Warming Relations
Indian Affairs Minister Jean Chrétien is seen here with Chief Jim Shot Both Sides in 1970. The chief was the grandson of Red Crow, one of the original signatories to Treaty Seven, which involved most of what is now southern Alberta.

Shirley Williams:

"When I got out I didn't know who I was — Indian or not! I thought I was white or wanted to be white."

North American Indian Prison Camp by Cree Artist George Littlechild
The federal government's education policy changed from segregation to integration with non-Aboriginal children. Although residential schools remained in some remote areas, most were replaced with day schools.

Closing the Doors

Day schools were appealing to the government for several reasons. Day schools would cost the government less to run. Government officials thought that if the children spent the day with white children and then went home to their families, they could more easily pass on what they had learned to their parents. Aboriginal students would be more easily assimilated if they were going to school with other Canadian children. In 1969, First Nations groups began to regain control of their children's education and some began running their own schools. In 1982, Canada's constitution was enacted with a provision recognizing the rights of Indian, Metis, and Inuit peoples, which finally led to the closing of the final residential school in 1996.

The Sixties Scoop
After the church-run schools closed, governments continued to believe that Aboriginal people were incapable of parenting their children effectively. Rather than offering support or parenting classes, thousands of children were forcibly removed by child welfare authorities and placed in non-Aboriginal foster homes.

Blue Quills
This student demonstration was in support of a 1970 campaign to have the Blue Quills school in Edmonton, Alberta, turned over to a First Nations educational authority. After a twenty-one-day sit-in, Jean Chrétien met with the Blue Quills Native Education Council and agreed to allow them to run the school.

Native Teachers
When individual First Nations bands took control of their education system, Native teachers began to be employed. Students thrived and their culture and heritage became part of their education.

The White Paper Versus the Red Paper

In 1969, a government White Paper was released. It set out a plan to eliminate the Department of Indian Affairs and Native status. Prime Minister Pierre Elliot Trudeau's government didn't want there to be any distinct group of people in Canada; it wanted everyone to be treated equally. Trudeau and his Indian Affairs Minister Jean Chrétien set out their objective to assimilate First Nations people and eliminate any special treatment, such as reserve lands and their rights to hunt and fish. Aboriginal people were outraged and countered with the Red Paper, presented by Harold Cardinal, President of the Indian Association of Alberta. Under enormous pressure the government relented and withdrew their paper. This cartoon shows (left to right) Harold Cardinal wearing a headdress; George Manuel, President of the National Indian Brotherhood; Trudeau dressed as a king; and Jean Chrétien dressed as a knight in armour.

New Residential Schools

While the government was busy closing residential schools in most of Canada, they created some new and improved schools in the north. This school in James Bay was for First Nations, Inuit, and Metis children who lived too remotely to attend day schools.

Day School Policy

Pierre Elliott Trudeau was in power during the change from residential schools to day schools. He agreed to recognize the rights of Indian, Metis, and Inuit peoples when he brought Canada's constitution home in the Constitution Act of 1982.

The Last Residential School

Gordon's School, in Punnichy, Saskatchewan, was the last residential school to close its doors in 1996.

CHAPTER 6

LIFE AFTER RESIDENTIAL SCHOOL

The Struggle of Survivors

After being away from home for years and living in a European-style culture, Aboriginal children struggled to fit back into their communities. Survivors had little or no connection to their culture or, often, to their families. Many could no longer speak their native language. They were often psychologically damaged by their school experiences but there was no support system to help them cope. The resulting social problems within communities have been overwhelming.

Not My Girl
With the residential schools closing, students were finally able to go home. They soon found out that they didn't fit in there anymore. Many could no longer speak their language and they had lost the taste for the foods they grew up on. The Survivors returned feeling like outsiders.

Alice Blondin:

"I remember Mom and Dad's arrival in 1956. I was playing outside our yard when I was called to see someone. I saw an older, Native man and woman smiling at me with their arms stretched out to hold me. I remember seeing Mom and Dad but I could not remember who they were. They kissed me and hugged me, lifting me and squeezing me so hard. I remember this, but I felt strange, not knowing them because I was so young and hadn't seen them in years. I was unable to communicate with them due to our language barrier. By that age, I was already programmed not to speak Dene, not to feel, and not to cry."

We All Look Alike by Jaune Quick–to–See Smith

After leaving the horrors of attending residential schools behind, Survivors faced new challenges. Rampant racism targeted Aboriginal peoples. Depression among Survivors was common. How could they better themselves and provide for their families if they couldn't get a chance? Poverty, homelessness, violence, drug and alcohol abuse, sexual abuse, suicide, divorce, prostitution, and criminal activity became the legacy of many residential school Survivors.

I Cannot Speak by Phil Young

This artwork speaks of the depression and helplessness that Survivors felt. The post-traumatic stress disorder and suicidal thoughts that went hand-in-hand with the abuse suffered at school contributed to a continued cycle of violence, alcoholism, and drug abuse.

Depression among Survivors was common. How could they better them- selves and provide for their families if they couldn't get the chance?

Diana Blackman's Quilt Square

Diana Blackman was sent away to school when her mother was sent to prison. "The strongest feeling I have about going to residential school was being disconnected to my family. I believe that this disconnection has had a lasting affect with all of my relationships. I have had to work at it for many years and I still do to this day."

The Struggle of Survivors 87

Anger

Theodore Fontaine felt a great deal of anger toward his parents for what he felt was their abandonment of him. Not until he was older did he understand the hurt and guilt they felt at leaving him at school.

Theodore Fontaine:

> "I drew this picture as an adult, after I'd begun my healing journey. It depicts my being left at residential school a few days after my seventh birthday."

Marius Tungilik:

> "You could see the manifestations of dysfunction everywhere. There were people who tried to escape reality by drinking or doing drugs, through violence, misplaced anger, confusion, crime . . . The signs were everywhere. But no one talked about it."

Marius Tungilik

"We were told that we were Eskimos. We did not amount to anything. The only way we could succeed was to learn the English way of life. So in that sense it was psychologically degrading as well. We were made to hate our own people, basically, our own kind. We looked down on them because they did not know how to count in English, speak English or read or any of those things that we were now able to do. That's sick."

Peter Irniq

"So in 1964 I attended Churchill Vocational Centre and never got back to my home community. It's something that I'm sorry about. It's something I feel pretty bad about over the course of my past years."

"For my part, for myself, I became extremely embarrassed to be an Eskimo . . ."

— Peter Irniq

Poverty
Half of Canada's First Nations children live in poverty. In Saskatchewan and Manitoba, the rate is higher, at approximately two-thirds.

Table 5: Aboriginal Offender Population as of 31 December 2001

	Gender	National Total	Atlantic	Quebec	Ontario	Prairie	Pacific
First Nation	Female	128	9	3	15	91	10
	Male	2,219	91	99	339	1,269	421
Métis	Female	50	0	1	2	43	4
	Male	885	9	115	35	569	157
Inuit	Female	4	2	0	0	2	0
	Male	128	17	18	53	36	4

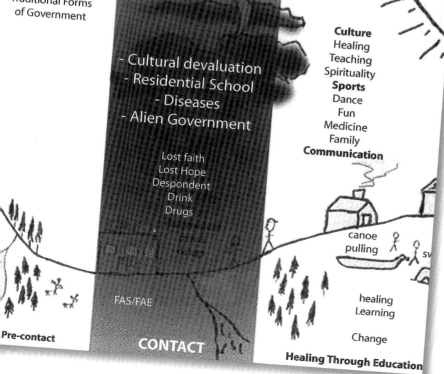

Traditional Forms of Government

- Cultural devaluation
- Residential School
- Diseases
- Alien Government

Lost faith
Lost Hope
Despondent
Drink
Drugs

FAS/FAE

Pre-contact

CONTACT

Culture
Healing
Teaching
Spirituality
Sports
Dance
Fun
Medicine
Family
Communication

canoe
pulling

sv

healing
Learning

Change

Healing Through Education

Doing Time
Although Aboriginal peoples make up only a small percentage of the Canadian population, 18 per cent of federal inmates in 2001 were Aboriginal. By 2013, the percentage had increased to 23.2.

Cycle of Healing
This is an illustration of the cycle of healing many First Nations communities face, created by the Aboriginal Health Foundation. It recommends healing through education, particularly cultural education.

The Struggle of Survivors

The Next Generations

The legacy of residential schools affected not only the Survivors, but the parents who were left behind, the partners of the Survivors, and the Survivors' children. Without the benefit of growing up in a family, many Survivors lacked parenting skills and were often neglectful and abusive toward their own children. Alcoholism became a common and intergenerational problem. The number of Aboriginal men in prison rose. The schools created a legacy of poverty, alcoholism, and abuse.

Alice Blondin (right) and her Daughters
Alice attended four different residential schools in the Northwest Territories. She stayed at St. Joseph's Roman Catholic Mission School in Fort Resolution, Breynat Hall in Fort Smith, Lapointe Hall in Fort Simpson, and Akaitcho Hall in Yellowknife.

"I saw my friends struggling with the effects of abuse, addicting themselves to cover up the pain. Some are still addicted to alcohol and drugs, but many have dealt with addictions only to find themselves caught by another addiction called 'swap addictions.' For example, practising sobriety but playing nightly bingo, or gambling, and so on. Some of my friends took prescription pills from year to year, for stress related to years of mental abuse.

"Today those affected by the intergenerational impacts of abuse in residential school include the students' children and grandchildren, who are layered with many dysfunctional behaviours. The north is a difficult place to heal, especially for those intergenerational children and grandchildren of residential schools Survivors that may be hooked on hard drugs. There are no treatment centres for that, nor is secondary treatment available when needed. Those resources are badly needed by Native people, north and south.

"Residential school was a government and Christian missionary initiative, and these same institutions now need to come up with treatment centres across Canada. So, if one Native person says, 'I need to get better and heal,' they'd better have a place to go. My friends and I have been on this difficult path for many years, teaching ourselves what the Grey Nuns neglected to teach us, struggling with daily living, and looking for jobs to sustain us in the future. There will always be hope for recovery but the government has to help us get out of this web we're caught in."

Abuse and Illness
Abraham Ruben attended the federal day school in Inuvik, Northwest Territories, for eleven years. "There are kids who are susceptible to alcohol and drug abuse, spousal abuse, physical abuse to others and I think there are a lot of illnesses that developed out of it. They become more susceptible to mental illness and psychological trauma." The above painting by artist Jim Logan is titled *Father Image 2*.

Lillian Elias:

"We drank a lot. We did drink a lot when my husband was alive and when I was a teenager I drank a lot because of that, not knowing who to turn to and not knowing who to talk to because a lot of people that I tried to talk to wouldn't understand me. They wouldn't even understand the situation that I went through."

Alcoholism

Many Survivors dealing with the trauma of abuse turned to alcohol and drugs. Shirley Flowers recalls her difficult past, "I had become an alcoholic. I started drinking when I was in the dorm. It took me a while to get over that. I had my first drink when I was thirteen years old."

Depression

Many Survivors did not tell their children about their residential school experiences. Children grew up not understanding why their parents were suffering from depression, addictions, and other problems.

" The impacts of the legacy of residential schools have not ended with those who attended the schools. They affected the Survivors' partners, their children, their grandchildren, their extended families, and their communities. Children who were abused in the schools sometimes went on to abuse others. Many students who spoke to the Commission said they developed addictions as a means of coping. "

Truth and Reconciliation
Commission of Canada

Volume One: Summary, p. 183–4

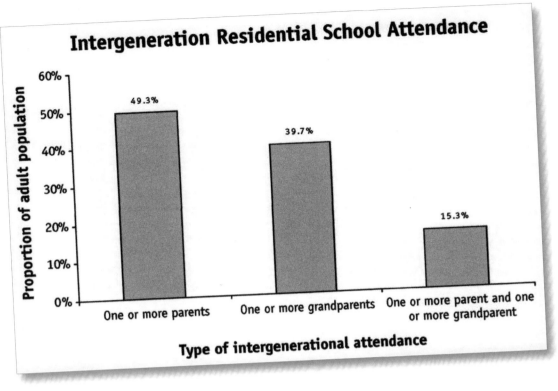

Intergeneration Residential School Attendance

Proportion of adult population (y-axis): 0% to 60%

- One or more parents: 49.3%
- One or more grandparents: 39.7%
- One or more parent and one or more grandparent: 15.3%

Type of intergenerational attendance (x-axis)

Intergenerational Impact

This graph from the First Nations Regional Longitudinal Health Survey shows the proportion of adults who have parents, grandparents, or both parents and grandparents who attended residential schools. As they grew older, former students became parents, but with no idea how to parent. Having been abused, many were abusive. Having never been shown love, they didn't know how to show love to their own children.

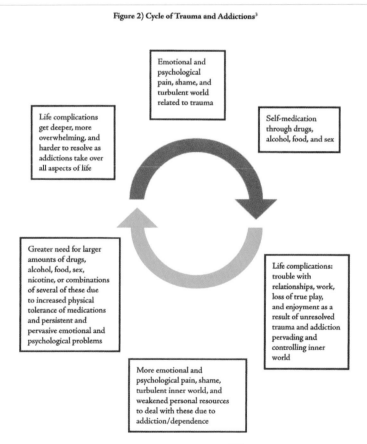

Figure 2) Cycle of Trauma and Addictions[3]

- Emotional and psychological pain, shame, and turbulent world related to trauma
- Self-medication through drugs, alcohol, food, and sex
- Life complications: trouble with relationships, work, loss of true play, and enjoyment as a result of unresolved trauma and addiction pervading and controlling inner world
- More emotional and psychological pain, shame, turbulent inner world, and weakened personal resources to deal with these due to addiction/dependence
- Greater need for larger amounts of drugs, alcohol, food, sex, nicotine, or combinations of several of these due to increased physical tolerance of medications and persistent and pervasive emotional and psychological problems
- Life complications get deeper, more overwhelming, and harder to resolve as addictions take over all aspects of life

Coming Out Ceremony

A coming out ceremony allows parents to proudly present their children to the community. The youngsters wear colourful regalia and join in their first traditional dance. Pictured here at their coming out ceremony are Cassandra Bisson, Kyleigh Biedermann, and Hanako Hubbard-Rudulovich in M'Chigeeng First Nation in Ontario.

Cycle of Trauma and Addiction

The trauma of being taken from their homes and families and sent to residential schools where so many children suffered abuse created a generation of adults who didn't know how to cope. Many Survivors used drugs and alcohol to dull the pain of what they had survived, which created a cycle of self-loathing and self-destructive behaviour.

Life after Residential School

Passing It On
The intergenerational impact of residential schools has had serious implications for the children and grandchildren of Survivors. Alcoholism and abuse are often passed down from generation to generation.

The intergenerational impact of residential schools has had serious implications for the children and grandchildren of Survivors.

The Next Generation
With so many Survivors missing out on an education, it has become more important for their children and grandchildren to get a good education.

Speaking Out

Tired of being ignored, Survivors began speaking out. One of the first to come forward to expose the abuse he suffered at residential school in Fort Alexander, Manitoba, was Phil Fontaine, a well-known activist, leader of the Association of Manitoba Chiefs, and future national chief of the Assembly of First Nations. He stunned the public with revelations of sexual, physical, and psychological abuse. He spoke about the intergenerational impact of the abused becoming abusers themselves. He urged churches to acknowledge the abuse that students suffered in residential schools.

Nora Bernard

Nora Bernard was nine when she was sent to the Shubenacadie Residential School in Nova Scotia. She attended the school for five years. In 1995, she began organizing former residential school students to file a class-action lawsuit. This lawsuit played a vital role in leading to the Indian Residential Schools Settlement Agreement.

Robert Joseph

Robert Joseph, a hereditary chief of the Gwa wa enuk First Nation, attended the Alert Bay, BC, residential school for eleven years. As the executive director of the BC-based Indian Residential School Survivors Society, he was involved in supporting former students. He campaigned for public recognition of the history and the continued impact of the residential school system.

Phil Fontaine

In 1990, Phil Fontaine revealed the physical and sexual abuse he experienced at a residential school in Manitoba. The experience drove him in his fight for redress for Aboriginal peoples.

> "In my grade three class, if there were 20 boys, every single one of them would have experienced what I experienced. They would have experienced some aspect of sexual abuse."

READ MORE

Call to Action!

In June 2007, Phil Fontaine spoke about the anger and frustration building in Aboriginal communities over the government's slow progress tackling important issues affecting Aboriginal peoples. Fontaine called for a peaceful National Day of Action to address urgent issues in Aboriginal communities, such as poor water quality, lack of education, and staggering poverty.

> "Our hope is that history records June 29 as a day of promise, one that affirms our shared goal of building a higher quality of life for First Nations people and a stronger Canada for all."

Read more at
http://tinyurl.com/rcwresidential02

Martha Joseph

A Survivor of the Port Alberni Residential School in BC, Martha Joseph suffered depression, alcoholism, and a fear of intimacy after the abuse she went through as a student. After several suicide attempts, Martha decided to take action for her fellow Survivors. In 2005 at the age of 67, Martha walked from Kelowna, BC, to Ottawa, ON, to raise awareness of residential school Survivors.

Survivors as Leaders

Despite their traumatic experiences, some Survivors of the residential school system have become leaders in their communities and across Canada. Aboriginal Canadians have become judges, educators, politicians, activists, authors, and artists. Many are involved in working toward reconciliation and acknowledgement, not only for the Survivors but for their families and communities.

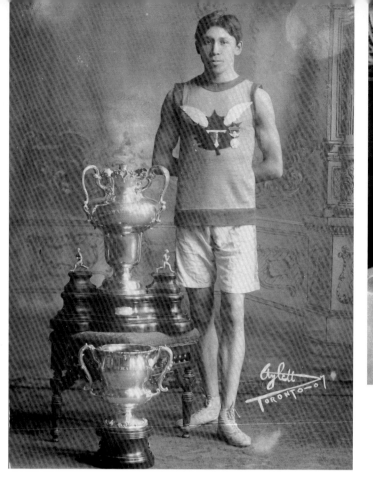

Tom Longboat
Tom Longboat was a legendary long distance runner from Brantford, Ontario. As a child, he attended the Mohawk Institute. He was an Olympian and a veteran of the First World War. He faced racism throughout his career. Newspapers called him a "redskin" and "the original dummy."

Tomson Highway
Tomson Highway is one of Canada's most prominent authors. He was born in a snowbank in Manitoba and spent most of his childhood (from the ages of six to fifteen) in Guy Hill Residential School. He is a playwright, a novelist, and a musician.

***The Raven and the First Men* by Bill Reid**
Bill Reid was considered one of Canada's greatest artists. A renowned carver, goldsmith, and sculptor, Reid was of Haida and European descent and the son of a residential school Survivor. His mother lost her language and any pride in her culture but when Bill Reid discovered Haida art, he embraced it.

Finding My Talk

Artist Agnes Smith created this self-portrait after meeting another woman at a powwow. No words were exchanged but they shared a pride in their culture and in the dance. This represents the importance of knowing who you are and where you belong.

Marius Tungilik

Marius Tungilik, left, is shown here as a boy in the early 1970s at Tusarvik School in Naujaat (Repulse Bay) in what is now Nunavut. He is a public speaker and is active in Inuit politics. He has spent many years promoting healing among his fellow Inuit residential school Survivors.

Acting against Injustice

In 2010, Aboriginal women marched against the injustices of the *Indian Act* on Aboriginal communities. Idle No More (www.idlenomore.ca) is a grassroots movement founded in December 2012 by four women. Its goals are sovereignty, land protection, and equality. It also seeks justice regarding Canada's missing and murdered Indigenous women.

Read More at
http://tinyurl.com/rcwresidential003

Jordin Tootoo

Jordin Tootoo was the first Inuit to play in the NHL. He faced racism and poverty and had to recover from the suicide of his brother, Terence.

National Forgiven Summit

As part of the healing process following the Government of Canada's official apology, a charter of forgiveness — signed by elders, Survivors, and Aboriginal youth — was presented to the Minister of Indian Affairs in 2010.

READ MORE

Survivors as Leaders

CHAPTER 7

APOLOGY AND REDRESS

The Government Apologizes

"The treatment of children in Indian Residential Schools is a sad chapter in our history."

After years of lobbying and drawing public attention to the horrific abuse in the schools, authorities finally accepted responsibility for the consequences of their policies and actions. First, the RCMP apologized for its role in taking the children. In 2007, the Canadian government entered into the Indian Residential Schools Settlement Agreement (IRS) to settle the lawsuits against it. The agreement included payment to residential school Survivors, compensation for victims of abuse, funding for healing and commemoration projects, and the formation of the Truth and Reconciliation Commission (TRC). Then, on June 11, 2008, Survivors of the residential schools finally received an apology from the Canadian government. Five Aboriginal leaders and six residential school Survivors were invited to witness the apology.

RCMP Apology, May 2004
"Many aboriginal people have found the courage to step outside of that legacy of this terrible chapter in Canadian history to share their stories. You heard one of those stories today. To those of you who suffered tragedies at residential schools we are very sorry for your experience. We, I, as Commissioner of the RCMP, am truly sorry for what role we played in the residential school system and the abuse that took place in that system."

TORONTO STAR

thestar.com

LET ME COUNT THE NAYS
Bestseller lists 40 reasons not to have children
LIVING — L1

LEFT SPEECHLESS
Citytv to pull plug on Speakers Corner
ENT — E1

ARE LEAFS WAITING FOR BURKE?
Fletcher to keep seat warm till '09
SPORTS — S1

'We are sorry'

Tears fall in hushed House of Commons as Prime Minister apologizes on behalf of nation for residential schools ordeal

Assembly of First Nations national chief Phil Fontaine is hugged by his daughter Maya after Prime Minister Stephen Harper...

Fraud has TTC set to get rid of tickets

Tokens would replace adult tickets by fall

DANIEL DALE
STAFF REPORTER

The TTC has proposed the replacement of adult tickets with tokens by the end of September in order to combat increasingly effective counterfeiters.

The transit authority announced at the same time, that one of its own ticket collectors was arrested Tuesday night after counterfeit tickets were sold from her booth at Wilson and...

THE GLOBE AND MAIL
CANADA'S NATIONAL NEWSPAPER

NATIVE RESIDENTIAL SCHOOLS » FROM THE FLOOR OF THE HOUSE OF COMMONS, THE PRIME MINISTER APOLOGIZES

TON HANSON/THE CANADIAN PRESS

> The government of Canada built an educational system in which very young children were often forcibly removed from their homes, often taken far from their communities. Many were inadequately fed, clothed and housed. All were deprived of the care and nurturing of their parents, grandparents and communities. First Nations, Inuit and Métis languages and cultural practices were prohibited in these schools. Tragically, some of these children died while attending residential schools and others never returned home. ...

We are sorry "

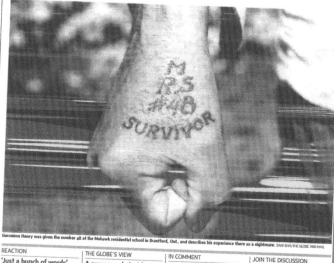

Geronimo Henry was given the number 48 at the Mohawk residential school in Brantford, Ont., and describes his experience there as a nightmare. SAMI SIVA/THE GLOBE AND MAIL

BY BILL CURRY AND GLORIA GALLOWAY OTTAWA

Prime Minister Stephen Harper had yet to utter a single word of Canada's apology to former Indian residential schools students when the cheering began. Native drumming and shouts turned into loud, simultaneous clapping. Raw emotion bursting for an apology decades overdue. There were many smiles.

For the sexual and physical abuse that occurred at the schools, Canada apologized. For the efforts to wipe out aboriginal languages and culture in the name of assimilation, Mr. Harper expressed remorse.

But aboriginal eyes in the now quiet House of Commons room began to tear when the Prime Minister acknowledged the ongoing, generational impacts of residential schools.

"We now recognize that, in separating children from their families, we undermined the ability of many to adequately parent their own children and sowed the seeds for generations to follow," he said. "Not only did you suffer these abuses as children, but as you became parents, you were powerless to protect your own children from suffering the same experience, and for this we are sorry."

Known as the generational effect of the schools, it is the lesser-told story. Many children who never set foot in one have grown up with parents who never learned that children need hugs. Some grew up with parents and relatives who learned the ways of abuse at the schools.

"You have been working on recovering from this experience for a long time and in a very real sense, we are now joining you on this journey," Mr. Harper concluded. "The government of Canada sincerely apologizes and asks the forgiveness of aboriginal peoples for failing them so badly."

Unlike Australian Prime Minister Kevin Rudd in his apology to aboriginals in February, Mr. Harper made no promises to improve aboriginal social conditions.

» SEE SCHOOLS: PAGE 8

REACTION
'Just a bunch of words'
For Geronimo Henry, 71, the apology is too little, too late. Read about his experience at a residential school, as well as that of nearly a dozen others.
NEWS, PAGES 8-9 ◆

THE GLOBE'S VIEW
A process only just begun
No longer mired in the past, Canada must now turn its attention to the sins of the present: entrenched dependency, abject poverty and unsettled land claims.
EDITORIAL, PAGE 16 ◆

IN COMMENT
Whither reconciliation?
Canada has spent billions and the biggest winners have been the lawyers. What could that money have bought if we'd paid it forward instead of back?
MARGARET WENTE, PAGE 17 ◆

JOIN THE DISCUSSION
GlobeSalon kicks off
In a new online feature, Margaret MacMillan, Michael Adams and other luminaries discuss the PM's apology beginning today at 9 a.m. (ET).
GLOBEANDMAIL.COM ◆

The Government Apologizes

99

At Long Last
Canada's Aboriginal leaders, along with a number of former residential school students, were present on the floor of the House of Commons for the 2008 residential school apology. Clockwise from left: former student Don Favel; former student Mary Moonias; former student Mike Cachagee, President of the National Residential School Survivors Society; former student Crystal Merasty; former student Peter Irniq; Mary Simon, President of the Inuit Tapiriit Kanatami; Phil Fontaine, National Chief of the Assembly of First Nations; Beverly Jacobs, President of the Native Women's Association of Canada; Clem Chartier, President of the Metis National Council.

"We heard the Government of Canada take full responsibility for this dreadful chapter in our shared history. We heard the prime minister declare that this will never happen again. Finally, we heard Canada say it is sorry. Brave Survivors, through the telling of their painful stories, have stripped white supremacy of its authority and legitimacy." — Phil Fontaine

Finally Acknowledged

Survivors and their families had waited years for the government to take responsibility for its role in the residential schools. June 11, 2008, was an important day for many of them. Prime Minister Harper is seen here with Chuck Strahl, the Minister of Indian Affairs and Northern Development at the time.

Responsibility

Stephen Harper and Phil Fontaine pose for the cameras after the historic apology.

The Government of Canada Apologizes

Following is the full text of the apology given by the Prime Minister of Canada on behalf of the Government of Canada in the Canadian Parliament on June 11, 2008.

The treatment of children in Indian Residential Schools is a sad chapter in our history.

For more than a century, Indian Residential Schools separated over 150,000 Aboriginal children from their families and communities. In the 1870s, the federal government, partly in order to meet its obligation to educate Aboriginal children, began to play a role in the development and administration of these schools. Two primary objectives of the Residential Schools system were to remove and isolate children from the influence of their homes, families, traditions and cultures, and to assimilate them into the dominant culture. These objectives were based on the assumption Aboriginal cultures and spiritual beliefs were inferior and unequal. Indeed, some sought, as it was infamously said, "to kill the Indian in the child." Today, we recognize that this policy of assimilation was wrong, has caused great harm, and has no place in our country.

One hundred and thirty-two federally-supported schools were located in every province and territory, except Newfoundland, New Brunswick and Prince Edward Island. Most schools were operated as "joint ventures" with Anglican, Catholic, Presbyterian or United Churches. The Government of Canada built an educational system in which very young children were often forcibly removed from their homes, often taken far from their communities. Many were inadequately fed, clothed and housed. All were deprived of the care and nurturing of their parents, grandparents and communities. First Nations, Inuit and Metis languages and cultural practices were prohibited in these schools. Tragically, some of these children died while attending residential schools and others never returned home.

The government now recognizes that the consequences of the Indian Residential Schools policy were profoundly negative and that this policy has had a lasting and damaging impact on Aboriginal culture, heritage and language. While some former students have spoken positively about their experiences at residential schools, these stories are far overshadowed by tragic accounts of the emotional, physical and sexual abuse and neglect of helpless children, and their separation from powerless families and communities.

The legacy of Indian Residential Schools has contributed to social problems that continue to exist in many communities today.

It has taken extraordinary courage for the thousands of Survivors that have come forward to speak publicly about the abuse they suffered. It is a testament to their resilience as individuals and to the strength of their cultures. Regrettably, many former students are not with us today and died never having received a full apology from the Government of Canada.

The government recognizes that the absence of an apology has been an impediment to healing and reconciliation. Therefore, on behalf of the Government of Canada and all Canadians, I stand before you, in this Chamber so central to our life as a country, to apologize to Aboriginal peoples for Canada's role in the Indian Residential Schools system.

To the approximately 80,000 living former students, and all family members and communities, the Government of Canada now recognizes that it was wrong to forcibly remove children from their homes and we apologize for having done this. We now recognize that it was wrong to separate children from rich and vibrant cultures and traditions, that it created a void in many lives and communities, and we apologize for having done this. We now recognize that, in separating children from their families, we undermined the ability of many to adequately parent their own children and sowed the seeds for generations to follow, and we apologize for having done this. We now recognize that, far too often, these institutions gave rise to abuse or neglect and were inadequately controlled, and we apologize for failing to protect you. Not only did you suffer these abuses as children, but as you became parents, you were powerless to protect your own children from suffering the same experience, and for this we are sorry.

The burden of this experience has been on your shoulders for far too long. The burden is properly ours as a Government, and as a country. There is no place in Canada for the attitudes that inspired the Indian Residential Schools system to ever prevail again. You have been working on recovering from this experience for a long time and in a very real sense, we are now joining you on this journey. The Government of Canada sincerely apologizes and asks the forgiveness of the Aboriginal peoples of this country for failing them so profoundly.

Nous le regrettons
We are sorry
Nimitataynan
Niminchinowesamin
Mamiattugut

In moving towards healing, reconciliation and resolution of the sad legacy of Indian Residential Schools, implementation of the Indian Residential Schools Settlement Agreement began on September 19, 2007. Years of work by Survivors, communities, and Aboriginal organizations culminated in an agreement that gives us a new beginning and an opportunity to move forward together in partnership.

A cornerstone of the Settlement Agreement is the Indian Residential Schools Truth and Reconciliation Commission. This Commission presents a unique opportunity to educate all Canadians on the Indian Residential Schools system. It will be a positive step in forging a new relationship between Aboriginal peoples and other Canadians, a relationship based on the knowledge of our shared history, a respect for each other and a desire to move forward together with a renewed understanding that strong families, strong communities and vibrant cultures and traditions will contribute to a stronger Canada for all of us.

On behalf of the Government of Canada

The Right Honourable
Stephen Harper,
Prime Minister of Canada

Watch the speech at
http://tinyurl.com/rcwresidential010

The Churches Apologize

One by one, the United Church of Canada, the Missionary Oblates of Mary Immaculate, the Anglican Church of Canada, and the Presbyterian Church of Canada issued formal apologies to the Survivors of the residential schools. In 2009, Pope Benedict XVI met privately with Chief Fontaine and expressed his sorrow for the abuse that the students suffered. Although the Catholic Church was responsible for 70 per cent of residential schools, the Canadian Conference of Catholic Bishops did not offer an apology. Nor did successive Catholic popes.

Anglican Church Apology
On August 6, 1993, the Anglican Church issued the first apology to the Survivors of the residential schools and addressed their role in the tragedy.

ANGLICAN OF CANADA

Apology to Native People

A message from the Primate, Archbishop Michael Peers, to the National Native Convocation Minaki, Ontario, Friday, August 6, 1993

My Brothers and Sisters:

Together here with you I have listened as you have told your stories of the residential schools.

I have heard the voices that have spoken of pain and hurt experienced in the schools, and of the scars which endure to this day.

I have felt shame and humiliation as I have heard of suffering inflicted by my people, and as I think of the part our church played in that suffering.

I am deeply conscious of the sacredness of the stories that you have told and I hold in the highest honour those who have told them.

I have heard with admiration the stories of people and communities who have worked at healing, and I am aware of how much healing is needed.

I also know that I am in need of healing, and my own people are in need of healing, and our church is in need of healing. Without that healing, we will continue the same attitudes that have done such damage in the past.

I also know that healing takes a long time, both for people and for communities.

I also know that it is God who heals, and that God can begin to heal when we open ourselves, our wounds, our failures and our shame to God. I want to take one step along that path here and now.

I accept and I confess before God and you, our failures in the residential schools. We failed you. We failed ourselves. We failed God.

I am sorry, more than I can say, that we were part of a system which took you and your children from home and family.

I am sorry, more than I can say, that we tried to remake you in our image, taking from you your language and the signs of your identity.

I am sorry, more than I can say, that in our schools so many were abused physically, sexually, culturally and emotionally.

On behalf of the Anglican Church of Canada, I present our apology.

Anglican Church Apology
"I accept and I confess before God and you, our failures in the residential schools. We failed you. We failed ourselves. We failed God.

I am sorry, more than I can say, that we were part of a system which took you and your children from home and family.

I am sorry, more than I can say, that we tried to remake you in our image, taking from you your language and the signs of your identity.

I am sorry, more than I can say, that in our schools so many were abused physically, sexually, culturally, and emotionally.

On behalf of the Anglican Church of Canada, I present our apology."

United Church Apology
The United Church issued an apology in 1986 for their aggressive attempts to eliminate Aboriginal spirituality and culture. In 1998, they gave another apology directly related to the residential schools. "To those individuals who were physically, sexually, and mentally abused as students of the Indian Residential Schools in which The United Church of Canada was involved, I offer you our most sincere apology. You did nothing wrong. You were and are the victims of evil acts that cannot under any circumstances be justified or excused."

LES MISSIONNAIRES OBLATS DE MARIE IMMACULÉE
THE MISSIONARY OBLATES OF MARY IMMACULATE

AN APOLOGY TO THE FIRST NATIONS OF CANADA BY THE OBLATE CONFERENCE OF CANADA

The Missionary Oblates of Mary Immaculate in Canada wish, after one hundred and fifty years of being with and ministering to the Native peoples of Canada, to offer an an apology for certain aspects of that presence and ministry.

A number of historical circumstances make this moment in history most opportune for this.

First, there is a symbolic reason. Next year, 1992, marks the five hundredth anniversary of the arrival of Europeans on the shores of America. As large scale celebrations are being prepared to mark this occasion, the Oblates of Canada wish, through this apology, to show solidarity with many Native people in Canada whose history has been adversely affected by this event. Anthropological and sociological insights of the late 20th century have shown how deep, unchallenged, and damaging was the naive cultural, ethnic, linguistic, and religious superiority complex of Christian Europe when its peoples met and interrelated with the aboriginal peoples of North America.

As well, recent criticisms of Indian residential schools and the exposure of instances of physical and sexual abuse within these schools call for such an apology.

Given this history, Native peoples and other groups alike are realizing that a certain healing needs to take place before a new and more truly cooperative phase of history can occur. This healing cannot however happen until some very complex, long-standing, and deep historical issues have been addressed.

It is in this context, and with a renewed pledge to be in solidarity with Native peoples in a common struggle for justice, that we, the Oblates of Canada, offer this apology:

We apologize for the part we played in the cultural, ethnic, linguistic, and religious imperialism that was part of the mentality with which the peoples of Europe first met the aboriginal peoples and which consistently has lurked behind the way the Native peoples of Canada have been treated by civil governments and by the churches. We were, naively, part of this mentality and were, in fact, often a key player in its implementation. We recognize that this mentality has, from the beginning, and ever since, continually threatened the cultural, linguistic, and religious traditions of the Native peoples.

Catholic Oblate Apology

Although the Catholic Church has never formally apologized, the Missionary Oblates of Mary Immaculate did issue an apology. In addition to their addressing the abuse and their part in it, the Oblates also apologized for dismissing the importance of the Aboriginal culture.

"Finally, we wish to apologize as well for our past dismissal of many of the riches of Native religious tradition. We broke some of your peace pipes and we considered some of your sacred practices as pagan and superstitious."

"We never thought for a moment we would be here to be received by the Holy Father to talk about an experience that has caused so much pain and suffering with so many."

— Phil Fontaine

Pope Benedict XVI

Although the Catholic Church did not issue an apology, Pope Benedict expressed his "sorrow" in a private meeting with Phil Fontaine and other Native representatives. Although the word "apology" wasn't used, Fontaine still considered this a significant statement. The Pope expressed that "acts of abuse cannot be tolerated in society," and "offered his sympathy and prayerful solidarity."

The Truth and Reconciliation Commission

Established in 2008 as an outcome of the IRS agreement between the Government of Canada and Survivors of the residential schools, the Truth and Reconciliation Commission of Canada (TRC) was set up as an independent body to investigate and report on the truth regarding the residential school system. It was also charged with recommending how Canada can achieve reconciliation between Aboriginal and non-Aboriginal Canadians in light of the harm the residential school system caused.

Truth and Reconciliation Commission of Canada

TRC Mandate

The role of the TRC was to document the stories of Survivors and anyone affected by the residential schools, and to educate all Canadians about this chapter in our history. The commission of three was headed by the Honourable Justice Murray Sinclair. The commissioners travelled across Canada, conducting hearings where Survivors could come and share their residential school experiences. Part of the goal was to begin a new path of understanding between Indigenous and non-Indigenous peoples.

Zapiro Cartoon

The path to reconciliation is a difficult one. The TRC states, "Canada's relationship with Aboriginal peoples has suffered as a result of the [residential schools]. Healing and repairing that relationship will require education, awareness, and increased understanding of the legacy and the impacts still being felt for everyone involved in that relationship."

TRC Commissioners
Commissioner Marie Wilson,
Chairperson Justice Murray Sinclair, and
Commissioner Chief Wilton Littlechild.

TRC Sacred Fire
At the beginning of every TRC
event, a sacred fire was lit. Ashes
from the last fire were added
and attendees of the event could
make offerings of tobacco or sage.
The smoke rising up from the
sacred fire signified their prayers
rising up. A fire keeper was
entrusted with keeping the fire lit
during the event.

READ
MORE

Port Alberni Statement Gathering Hearing
"I'm terrified to be here, because I was so
tormented here," cried one Survivor, who told
Commissioner Marie Wilson she had three
abusers at the school.

Another Survivor, George August, said,
"There is a building on this ground that terrifies
me. One of the supervisors used to take us in
there, put us in the tub and sexually abuse us. He
would make us do things to him . . . I can still
see, smell [and] taste it."

Read more at
http://tinyurl.com/rcwresidential01

The Truth and Reconciliation Commission

Reconciliation Week in Vancouver, BC
"As thousands participated in a week of events surrounding the Truth and Reconciliation Commission hearings, including the canoe event, many expressed hope for healing the broken relationship with Canadians. But for many Survivors, the anger remains," wrote David P. Ball for *Windspeaker*.

Irene Stevens:
"It's been a lot of turmoil for me and my family. I even see the hurt in my grandchildren. It's been really tough, especially when it affects my grandchildren. We tried so hard to keep them away from all these hurts."

Bentwood Box

This bentwood box was created by Coast Salish artist Luke Marston. The box incorporates stories of his grandmother's time at the school at Kuper Island, BC. As a child she was thrown down the stairs by a nun and broke her fingers. Never properly cared for, they healed in "a cramped position." "I remember seeing that as a child but I never knew the reason why her hands were like that," said Marston. This side of the box shows his grandmother holding her hands up, her fingers bent. The box was made from a single piece of red cedar that Marston steamed and bent into shape. It was used to collect gifts from Survivors.

TRC National Events

"What you are offering today is extremely valuable, not only to yourselves, not only to your families but for the generations yet to come," said TRC Commissioner Marie Wilson at one of the TRC national events, speaking both of the gifts that were deposited into the bentwood box and the testimony. She assured that it all would be made accessible to generations to come in the national research centre "so no one can say they didn't know" about the residential school era.

Missing Children Project

In 2008, the TRC launched a project to document the deaths and burial places of children who died while attending a residential school. To date the Missing Children Project has identified more than 3,000 children.

Justice Sinclair stated, "It is a time-consuming effort, but I think at the end of the day we will probably be able to do that for most of the children and ensure that our search of the records also will tell us whether the families were ever informed and what the families were told."

25

THE Missing Children PROJECT

PHOTO: Residential School students assemble at a cemetery in Fort George, 1946. Archives Deschâtelets

Working with Survivors and Aboriginal organizations, the TRC's Missing Children Project is documenting the deaths and the burial places of children who died while attending a residential school. To date, the TRC has identifed the names of, or information about, more than 3000 childern who died of disease or accident.

Visit the Missing Children booth in the Learning Place.

PHOTO: Asleep on the boat on the way to residential school in Fort George. Archives Deschâtelets

trc.

Coming to Terms with Our History

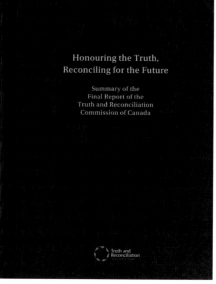

Honouring the Truth,
Reconciling for the Future

Summary of the
Final Report of the
Truth and Reconciliation
Commission of Canada

Truth and
Reconciliation

The Truth and Reconciliation Commission had the responsibility for discovering and documenting the truth about the historical experiences of Aboriginal peoples, and specifically about the residential school system. Their work was completed in 2015, and the commission made its findings available to all. First came a summary report, bringing together the results of hearings held across Canada, testimony of Survivors and others with knowledge of the school experience, and extensive research by historians.

Cultural genocide

The commission summarized its findings regarding the true history of the residential school system and the policies and attitudes it reflected by setting out the concept of cultural genocide.

" For over a century, the central goals of Canada's Aboriginal policy were to eliminate Aboriginal governments; ignore Aboriginal rights; terminate the Treaties; and, through a process of assimilation, cause Aboriginal peoples to cease to exist as distinct legal, social, cultural, religious, and racial entities in Canada. The establishment and operation of residential schools were a central element of this policy, which can best be described as 'cultural genocide.' *Physical genocide* is the mass killing of the members of a targeted group, and *biological genocide* is the destruction of the group's reproductive capacity. *Cultural genocide* is the destruction of those structures and practices that allow the group to continue as a group. States that engage in cultural genocide set out to destroy the political and social institutions of the targeted group. Land is seized, and populations are forcibly transferred and their movement is restricted. Languages are banned. Spiritual leaders are persecuted, spiritual practices are forbidden, and objects of spiritual value are confiscated and destroyed. And, most significantly to the issue at hand, families are disrupted to prevent the transmission of cultural values and identity from one generation to the next. In its dealing with Aboriginal people, Canada did all these things. "

Volume One: Summary, p. 1

Residential Schools and Other Government Measures

" The history of residential schools presented in this report commenced by placing the schools in the broader history of the global European colonization of Indigenous peoples and their lands. Residential schooling was only a part of the colonization of Aboriginal people. The policy of colonization suppressed Aboriginal culture and languages, disrupted Aboriginal government, destroyed Aboriginal economies, and confined Aboriginal people to marginal and often unproductive land. When that policy resulted in hunger, disease, and poverty, the federal government failed to meet its obligations to Aboriginal people. That policy was dedicated to eliminating Aboriginal peoples as distinct political and cultural entities and must be described for what it was: a policy of cultural genocide. "

Volume One: Summary, p. 133

Why This Policy? Why These Actions?

The research of the Truth and Reconciliation Commission led to these conclusions about the reasons for the policies and actions of government, churches, and social institutions:

Gain Land and Resources

" The Canadian government pursued this policy of cultural genocide because it wished to divest itself of its legal and financial obligations to Aboriginal people and gain control over their land and resources. If every Aboriginal person had been 'absorbed into the body politic,' there would be no reserves, no Treaties, and no Aboriginal rights. "
Volume One: Summary, p. 3

Superiority of European Civilization and Christian Religion

" The residential school system was based on an assumption that European civilization and Christian religions were superior to Aboriginal culture, which was seen as being savage and brutal. "
Volume One: Summary, p. 4

Aboriginal People Deemed Unfit Parents

" In establishing residential schools, the Canadian government essentially declared Aboriginal people to be unfit parents. "
Volume One: Summary, p. 4

The Impact of This Approach

" Despite the coercive measures that the government adopted, it failed to achieve its policy goals. Although Aboriginal peoples and cultures have been badly damaged, they continue to exist. Aboriginal people have refused to surrender their identity. "
Volume One: Summary, p. 6

A Shared Understanding of Canadian History

Many prominent Canadians have adopted the concept of cultural genocide as an appropriate and accurate term to describe government policies and measures towards Aboriginal peoples.

"The most glaring blemish on the Canadian historic record relates to our treatment of the First Nations that lived here at the time of colonization. An initial period of cooperative inter-reliance grounded in norms of equality and mutual dependence (described eloquently by John Raulston Saul in his book *A Fair Country*), was supplanted in the nineteenth century by the ethos of exclusion and cultural annihilation. Early laws forbade treaty Indians from leaving allocated reservations. Starvation and disease were rampant. Indians were denied the right to vote. Religious and social traditions, like the Potlatch and the Sun Dance, were outlawed. Children were taken from their parents and sent away to residential schools, where they were forbidden to speak their native languages, forced to wear white-man's clothing, forced to observe Christian religious practices, and not infrequently subjected to sexual abuse. The objective was to 'take the Indian out of the child,' and thus to solve what John A. Macdonald referred to as the 'Indian problem.' 'Indianness' was not to be tolerated; rather it must be eliminated. In the buzzword of the day, assimilation; in the language of the twenty-first century, cultural genocide.

We now understand that the policy of assimilation was wrong and that the only way forward is acknowledgement and acceptance of the distinct values, traditions, and religions of the descendants of the original inhabitants of the land we call Canada. In a moving ceremony in Parliament in 2008, the Prime Minister formally apologized to Canada's First Nation people for the abuses of the residential school system. A truth and reconciliation commission, whose report is about to be released, was established. Yet the legacy of intolerance lives on in the lives of First Nation people and their children — a legacy of too much poverty, too little education, and over-representation of Aboriginal people in our courts."

— Supreme Court of Canada Chief Justice Beverley McLachlin in a speech delivered May 28, 2015

Watch the speech at http://tinyurl.com/rcwresidential011

We Are All Treaty People

The Truth and Reconciliation Commission pointed out that the treaties negotiated on behalf of the British Crown and, later, the Canadian government with Aboriginal peoples contain commitments made on behalf of both parties. Every Canadian, Aboriginal and non-Aboriginal, is a party to these agreements.

" By virtue of the historical and modern Treaties negotiated by our government, we are all Treaty people. "
Volume One: Summary, p. 8

" Whether one is First Nations, Inuit, Metis, a descendant of European settlers, a member of a minority group that suffered historical discrimination in Canada, or a new Canadian, we all inherit both the benefits and obligations of Canada. We are all Treaty people who share responsibility for taking action on reconciliation. "
Volume One: Summary, p. 12

Calls to Action

In the first volume of its final report published in 2015, the Truth and Reconciliation Commission presented ninety-four calls to action on the part of governments, churches, institutions, and Canadian citizens as the plan for reconciliation between Aboriginal and non-Aboriginal Canadians. These are detailed in the report. Among them:

Child Welfare

" We call upon the federal, provincial, territorial, and Aboriginal governments to commit to reducing the number of Aboriginal children in care by:

    i.   Monitoring and assessing neglect investigations.

    ii. Providing adequate resources to enable Aboriginal communities and child-welfare organizations to keep Aboriginal families together where it is safe to do so, and to keep children in culturally appropriate environments, regardless of where they reside.

    iii. Ensuring that social workers and others who conduct child-welfare investigations are properly educated and trained about the history and impacts of residential schools.

    iv. Ensuring that social workers and others who conduct child-welfare investigations are properly educated and trained about the potential for Aboriginal communities and families to provide more appropriate solutions to family healing.

    v. Requiring that all child-welfare decision makers consider the impact of the residential school experience on children and their caregivers. "

Volume One: Summary, p. 319

Education

" We call upon the federal government to develop with Aboriginal groups a joint strategy to eliminate educational and employment gaps between Aboriginal and non-Aboriginal Canadians. "

Volume One: Summary, p. 320

Language and Culture

" We call upon the federal government to enact an Aboriginal Languages Act . . . "

Volume One: Summary, p. 321

" We call upon the federal government to acknowledge that Aboriginal rights include Aboriginal language rights. "

Volume One: Summary, p. 321

Health

❝ We call upon the federal, provincial, territorial, and Aboriginal governments to acknowledge that the current state of Aboriginal health in Canada is a direct result of previous Canadian government policies, including residential schools, and to recognize and implement the health-care rights of Aboriginal people as identified in international law, constitutional law, and under the Treaties. ❞

Volume One: Summary, p. 322

Justice

❝ We call upon federal, provincial, and territorial governments to commit to eliminating the overrepresentation of Aboriginal people in custody over the next decade, and to issue detailed annual reports that monitor and evaluate progress in doing so. ❞

Volume One: Summary, p. 324

❝ We call upon the federal, provincial, territorial, and Aboriginal governments to commit to eliminating the overrepresentation of Aboriginal youth in custody over the next decade. ❞

Volume One: Summary, p. 325

Alberni Indian Residential School Survivors
The Truth and Reconciliation Commission visited the Alberni Valley to gather statements from Survivors of the Alberni Residential School, one of the worst schools to operate in Canada.

Reconciliation

❝ We call upon federal, provincial, territorial, and municipal governments to fully adopt and implement the *United Nations Declaration on the Rights of Indigenous Peoples* as the framework for reconciliation. ❞

Volume One: Summary, p. 325

❝ We call upon the Government of Canada to develop a national action plan, strategies, and other concrete measures to achieve the goals of the *United Nations Declaration on the Rights of Indigenous Peoples.* ❞

Volume One: Summary, p. 325

Royal Proclamation and Covenant of Reconciliation

" We call upon the Government of Canada, on behalf of all Canadians, to jointly develop with Aboriginal peoples a Royal Proclamation of Reconciliation to be issued by the Crown. The proclamation would build on the Royal Proclamation of 1763 and the Treaty of Niagara of 1764, and reaffirm the nation-to-nation relationship between Aboriginal peoples and the Crown. "

Volume One: Summary, p. 326

" We call upon federal, provincial, territorial, and municipal governments to repudiate concepts used to justify European sovereignty over Indigenous peoples and lands, such as the Doctrine of Discovery and terra nullius, and to reform those laws, government policies, and litigation strategies that continue to rely on such concepts. "

Volume One: Summary, p. 327

National Council for Reconciliation

" We call upon the Parliament of Canada, in consultation and collaboration with Aboriginal peoples, to enact legislation to establish a National Council for Reconciliation. The legislation would establish the council as an independent, national, oversight body with membership jointly appointed by the Government of Canada and national Aboriginal organizations, and consisting of Aboriginal and non-Aboriginal members. "

Volume One: Summary, p. 328

Education and Curriculum

" We call upon the federal, provincial, and territorial governments, in consultation and collaboration with Survivors, Aboriginal peoples, and educators, to:

i. Make age-appropriate curriculum on residential schools, Treaties, and Aboriginal peoples' historical and contemporary contributions to Canada a mandatory education requirement for Kindergarten to Grade Twelve students.

ii. Provide the necessary funding to post-secondary institutions to educate teachers on how to integrate Indigenous knowledge and teaching methods into classrooms.

iii. Provide the necessary funding to Aboriginal schools to utilize Indigenous knowledge and teaching methods in classrooms.

iv. Establish senior-level positions in government at the assistant deputy minister level or higher dedicated to Aboriginal content in education. "

Volume One: Summary, p. 331

Missing Children and Burial Information

❝ We call upon all chief coroners and provincial vital statistics agencies that have not provided to the Truth and Reconciliation Commission of Canada their records on the deaths of Aboriginal children in the care of residential school authorities to make these documents available to the National Centre for Truth and Reconciliation. ❞

Volume One: Summary, p. 333

Commemoration

❝ We call upon the federal government, in collaboration with Aboriginal peoples, to establish, as a statutory holiday, a National Day for Truth and Reconciliation to honour Survivors, their families, and communities, and ensure that public commemoration of the history and legacy of residential schools remains a vital component of the reconciliation process. ❞

Volume One: Summary, p. 334-5

❝ We call upon the federal government, in collaboration with Survivors and their organizations, and other parties to the Settlement Agreement, to commission and install a publicly accessible, highly visible, Residential Schools National Monument in the city of Ottawa to honour Survivors and all the children who were lost to their families and communities. ❞

Volume One: Summary, p. 334-5

TRC Survivors Committee
Lottie May Johnson, a TRC Survivor Committee member speaks at the Circle of Reconciliation while Anglican Bishop Sue Moxley listens. Attendees were given the opportunity to share their experiences and talk about what reconciliation means to them.

Oath of Citizenship

❝ We call upon the Government of Canada to replace the Oath of Citizenship with the following:
I swear (or affirm) that I will be faithful and bear true allegiance to Her Majesty Queen Elizabeth II, Queen of Canada, Her Heirs and Successors, and that I will faithfully observe the laws of Canada including Treaties with Indigenous Peoples, and fulfill my duties as a Canadian citizen. ❞

Volume One: Summary, p. 337

Understanding — and Action: Next Steps

Following the publication of the Truth and Reconciliation Commission Final Report in June 2015, many voices were heard that supported the commission's call for a broad range of actions. A sampling of these responses show varying degrees of concrete commitments to action on the part of governments and institutions.

"The TRC's report provides recommendations to the Government of Canada concerning the IRS system and its terrible legacy. The TRC report maps a path forward to pursue reconciliation and renewed relationships with Aboriginal peoples based on a foundation of mutual understanding and respect. All levels of government, and indeed all Canadians, must work in partnership with First Nations and Aboriginal people to address the challenges faced by communities, including socio-economic gaps and healing. We must move toward our shared goal of reconciliation."

— *John Rustad, BC Minister of Aboriginal Relations and Reconciliation*

"While this is an important milestone in getting our country past the days of Indian residential schools, work is still needed to help heal the pain and restore trust from that wrong."
— *Prime Minister Stephen Harper*

"Though the Commission's work is coming to a close, this moment represents a beginning, not an end. As the TRC's report and recommendations note, it is time to act, without delay, to advance the process of reconciliation, and rebuild Canada's relationship with First Nations, Inuit, and Metis Peoples based on rights, respect, cooperation, and the standards of the *United Nations Declaration on the Rights of Indigenous Peoples*. Meaningful reconciliation will only come when we live up to our past promises and ensure the equality of opportunity required to create a fair and prosperous shared future."

— *Justin Trudeau,*
leader of the Liberal Party of Canada

"But if we do not teach all children and all Canadians the truth about colonization — the truth about Indigenous people helping Europeans survive and thrive, the truth about treaties, broken promises and broken families — if we do not teach these things, the patterns of distrust and disrespect so firmly entrenched by colonization and residential schools will continue to echo.

"Our journey of reconciliation encompasses many things: mourning, learning, understanding, healing. But ultimately, it is about respect. It is about walking together — walking together today to honour those who suffered the trauma of Canada's residential schools, and to thank you for sharing your experiences. And walking together into the future to build a strong partnership based on mutual respect and fairness."
— *Kathleen Wynne, Premier of Ontario*

"By recording the experiences of thousands of Survivors, the TRC has ensured that all Canadians can gain a deeper understanding of this dark chapter in our collective history, and of the devastating and lasting legacy it has left on Aboriginal Peoples' communities, cultures, languages, health, education, and welfare."
— *Justin Trudeau*

"Canada must show leadership and we must ensure that formal apologies made in 2008 were not in vain. The government must act immediately in the areas of education, child protection, and health care in order to put an end to the inequalities and sorry legacy of residential schools.

"We are determined to act upon the report of the Commission. We will consult with Indigenous people and establish which of the recommendations require the most pressing attention.

"Let us undertake to always pursue the truth, and to work together towards healing and reconciliation."

— *Tom Mulcair, leader of the federal New Democratic Party*

"Every citizen should learn our country's true shared history, from painful, shameful moments such as the residential schools and the Indian Act to uplifting moments like our original relationship — the promises we made to one another to share and live together in mutual respect and peaceful co-existence. Reconciliation means repairing our relationship by honouring those original promises.

"We must restore that original relationship of respect, partnership and sharing in the wealth of this land. Governments must respect our right to determine what happens in our traditional territories and our responsibility to care for the lands and waters. The government's legal duty to consult and accommodate us must be honoured and we must pursue the higher standard of free, prior and informed consent. Where we agree on development, revenue sharing is essential. This will help build stronger First Nations communities. We were not meant to be poor in our own homelands."

— *Perry Bellegarde,*
National Chief of Assembly of First Nations

Permanent Acknowledgements

Across the country there are monuments built to acknowledge and commemorate both the Survivors of the residential schools and those who never returned home. In addition, the TRC has called for a national monument to be erected in Ottawa.

LISTEN TO THE STORY

Where are the Children? Healing the Legacy of the Residential Schools

The exhibition *Where are the Children?* was developed to educate Canadians through personal stories, photos, and artifacts about the history of the residential schools and the impact that they continue to have on the Aboriginal population.

Listen to Survivors share their painful stories at http://tinyurl.com/rcwresidential04.

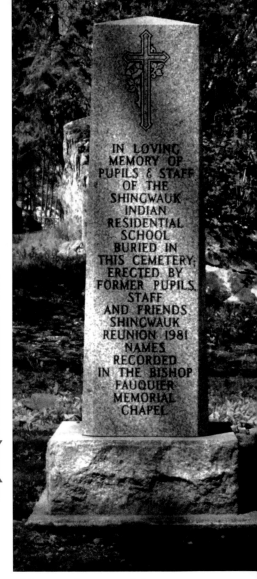

Shingwauk Memorial

A memorial to the forgotten children of Shingwauk at The Bishop Fauquier Chapel in Sault Ste. Marie, Ontario. Many children left for the school, never to return. The Children of Shingwauk Alumni Association strives to ensure that they are never forgotten.

THIS MONUMENT IS DEDICATED TO ALL CHILDREN FROM WALPOLE ISLAND HO ATTENDED RESIDENTIAL SCHOOLS OUGHOUT CANADA AND THE UNITED STATES OF AMERICA.

OM INSIDE THOSE WALLS ONE OUTSIDE HEARD CRIES: WHEN WE LEFT. NE HEARD OUR CRIES

Maam'pee day'aaw' meh, Kay'ah'beh (We Are Still Here)

The Walpole Island Residential School Memorial Monument is etched with 400 names of children from the Walpole Island First Nation who attended residential schools across Canada and the United States. Walpole Island is in southwestern Ontario.

Shingwauk Hall Historical Plaque

A plaque erected by the Ontario Heritage Foundation outside of the Bishop Fauquier Chapel in Sault Ste. Marie, where Shingwauk students had church services.

SHINGWAUK HALL

Shingwauk Hall was erected in 1935 to house a residential training school established in 1873 by the Reverend Edward F. Wilson. Under this Anglican missionary's tutelage the institution, named after the well-known Ojibway Chief Augustin Shingwauk (Little Pine), provided Indian children with religious instruction, occupational training and homemaking skills. The first frame structure, located at the nearby Garden River Reserve, was destroyed by fire within six days of its completion, and the foundation stone for a new three-storey stone building was laid here in 1874 by the Earl of Dufferin, the Governor-General of Canada. Other buildings were added, but of these the Bishop Fauquier Chapel, completed in 1883, is the sole remaining structure.

Looking Ahead

Christi Belcourt designed a stained glass window entitled "Giniigaaniimenaaning," which means "Looking Ahead." It was dedicated in a special ceremony on Parliament Hill on November 26, 2013. "The primary purpose of the window is to honour the First Nations, Metis, and Inuit children who attended Indian residential schools as well as their families and their communities who were impacted by the schools' legacy," said Minister John Duncan of Aboriginal Affairs and Northern Development Canada. "Through the official dedication of this window we honour your experiences and ensure they are never forgotten."

Signing Ceremony

As part of the Indian Residential Schools Settlement Agreement, a National Research Centre for Truth and Reconciliation was created at the University of Manitoba. The image above shows Justice Sinclair, centre, at the signing ceremony on June 21, 2013.

Urban Healing

In downtown Toronto, there is a rooftop oasis for the Aboriginal community that includes a sweat lodge and a healing circle, with a traditional fire box. Cedar, sweetgrass, and tobacco are part of the rooftop garden designed by Levitt Goodman architects.

Glooscap Educates the Community

Staff at the Glooscap Heritage Centre & Mi'kmaq Museum in Millbrook, Nova Scotia, teach Native and non-Native community members about Mi'kmaq culture. Millbrook is a successful band that is operating a number of local businesses, employing people, and embracing their heritage.

REACH Aboriginal Leadership Council

Rachelle Venne, CEO of the Institute for Advancement of Aboriginal Women, says, "We're teaching [young people] respect for their families, their Elders, their community, and most of all for themselves. We're helping them take a path in life that does not include crime, gangs, or drugs and that family violence is not the norm."

Timeline

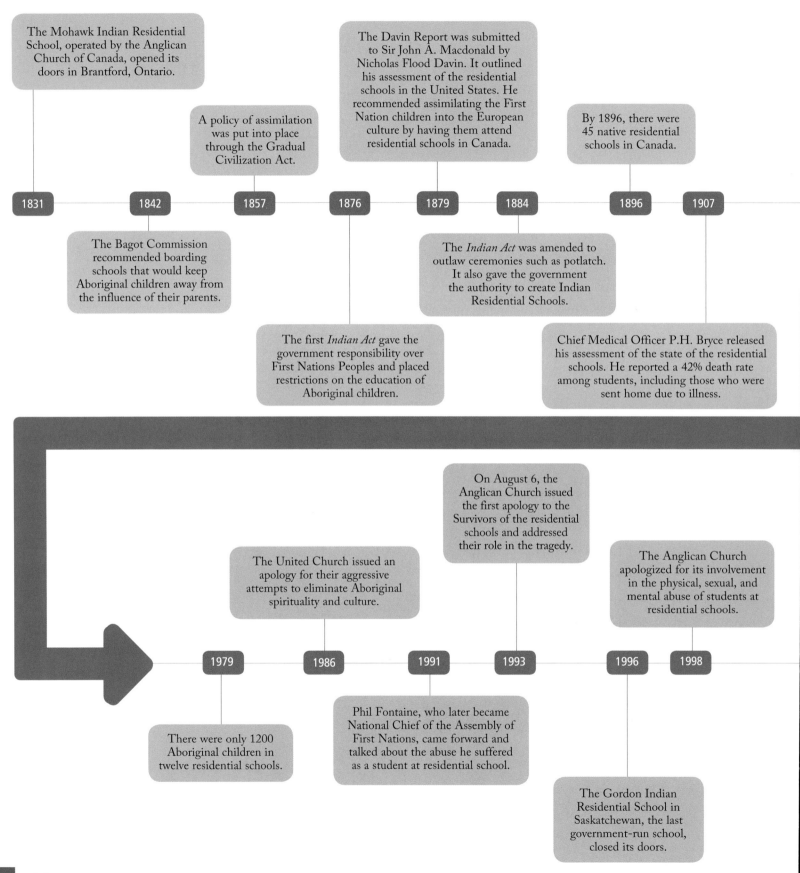

The Mohawk Indian Residential School, operated by the Anglican Church of Canada, opened its doors in Brantford, Ontario.

A policy of assimilation was put into place through the Gradual Civilization Act.

The Davin Report was submitted to Sir John A. Macdonald by Nicholas Flood Davin. It outlined his assessment of the residential schools in the United States. He recommended assimilating the First Nation children into the European culture by having them attend residential schools in Canada.

By 1896, there were 45 native residential schools in Canada.

1831　**1842**　**1857**　**1876**　**1879**　**1884**　**1896**　**1907**

The Bagot Commission recommended boarding schools that would keep Aboriginal children away from the influence of their parents.

The *Indian Act* was amended to outlaw ceremonies such as potlatch. It also gave the government the authority to create Indian Residential Schools.

The first *Indian Act* gave the government responsibility over First Nations Peoples and placed restrictions on the education of Aboriginal children.

Chief Medical Officer P.H. Bryce released his assessment of the state of the residential schools. He reported a 42% death rate among students, including those who were sent home due to illness.

On August 6, the Anglican Church issued the first apology to the Survivors of the residential schools and addressed their role in the tragedy.

The United Church issued an apology for their aggressive attempts to eliminate Aboriginal spirituality and culture.

The Anglican Church apologized for its involvement in the physical, sexual, and mental abuse of students at residential schools.

1979　**1986**　**1991**　**1993**　**1996**　**1998**

There were only 1200 Aboriginal children in twelve residential schools.

Phil Fontaine, who later became National Chief of the Assembly of First Nations, came forward and talked about the abuse he suffered as a student at residential school.

The Gordon Indian Residential School in Saskatchewan, the last government-run school, closed its doors.

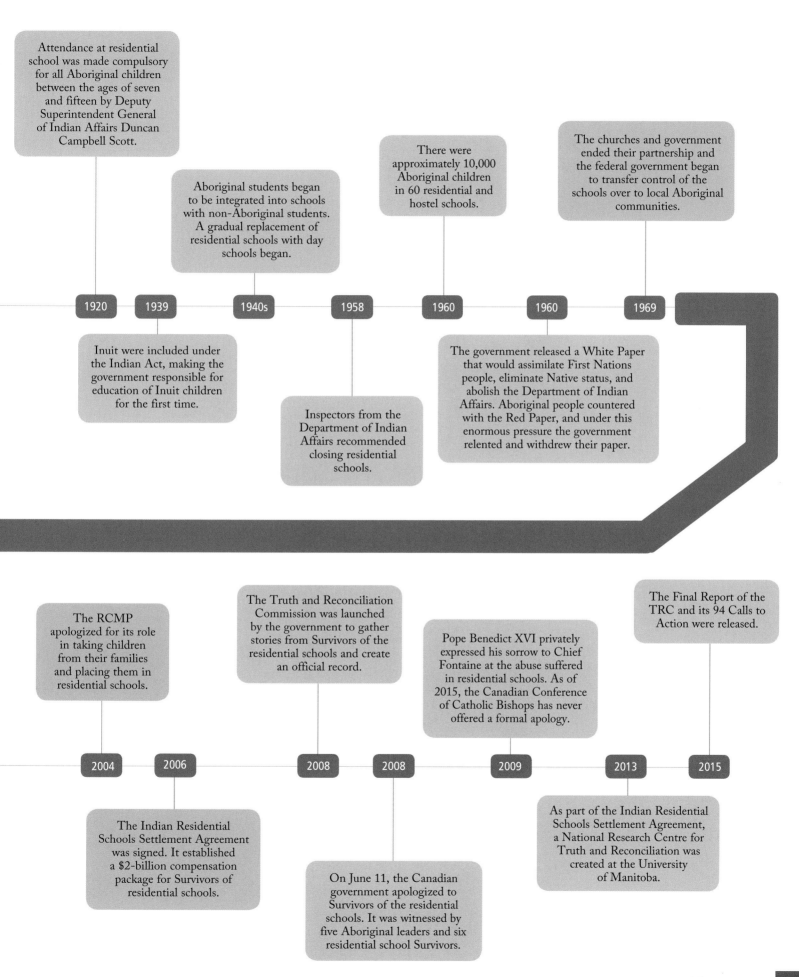

Attendance at residential school was made compulsory for all Aboriginal children between the ages of seven and fifteen by Deputy Superintendent General of Indian Affairs Duncan Campbell Scott.

Aboriginal students began to be integrated into schools with non-Aboriginal students. A gradual replacement of residential schools with day schools began.

There were approximately 10,000 Aboriginal children in 60 residential and hostel schools.

The churches and government ended their partnership and the federal government began to transfer control of the schools over to local Aboriginal communities.

1920   **1939**   **1940s**   **1958**   **1960**   **1960**   **1969**

Inuit were included under the Indian Act, making the government responsible for education of Inuit children for the first time.

Inspectors from the Department of Indian Affairs recommended closing residential schools.

The government released a White Paper that would assimilate First Nations people, eliminate Native status, and abolish the Department of Indian Affairs. Aboriginal people countered with the Red Paper, and under this enormous pressure the government relented and withdrew their paper.

The RCMP apologized for its role in taking children from their families and placing them in residential schools.

The Truth and Reconciliation Commission was launched by the government to gather stories from Survivors of the residential schools and create an official record.

Pope Benedict XVI privately expressed his sorrow to Chief Fontaine at the abuse suffered in residential schools. As of 2015, the Canadian Conference of Catholic Bishops has never offered a formal apology.

The Final Report of the TRC and its 94 Calls to Action were released.

2004   **2006**   **2008**   **2008**   **2009**   **2013**   **2015**

The Indian Residential Schools Settlement Agreement was signed. It established a $2-billion compensation package for Survivors of residential schools.

On June 11, the Canadian government apologized to Survivors of the residential schools. It was witnessed by five Aboriginal leaders and six residential school Survivors.

As part of the Indian Residential Schools Settlement Agreement, a National Research Centre for Truth and Reconciliation was created at the University of Manitoba.

Glossary

Assimilation: The culture of a minority or immigrant group becomes lost within another, more dominant, culture.

Bias: A preference or tendency to think or act in a certain way. Could be positive or negative.

Civil rights: The basic privileges that come with being a member of society in a certain country. Things such as a right to vote, to have an education, to receive justice in the courts.

Compensation: The payment of money to make up for a wrong that was done to a person or group.

Cultural genocide: Destroying anything that sets a group of people apart from another, such as language, tradition, and values.

Culture: The customs, traditions, and values of a country or its people.

Delegation: A small group of people who represent a much larger group's ideas or demands.

Discrimination: Unjust actions that are caused by a particular mindset or prejudice. A means of treating people negatively because of their group identity. Discrimination may be based on age, ancestry, gender, language, race, religion, political beliefs, sexual orientation, family status, physical or mental disability, appearance, or economic status. Acts of discrimination hurt, humiliate, and isolate the victim.

First Nations: Aboriginal Canadians who are neither Metis nor Inuit. There are currently over 600 First Nations communities in Canada.

Franchise: The right to vote. Aboriginal Canadians in British Columbia were denied the franchise — not allowed to vote — in provincial or federal elections until 1949. When someone's right to vote is taken away, they are disenfranchised.

Heritage: Traditions passed down to younger generations.

Immigration: The arrival of people into a country from their homeland.

Indian: Term formerly used to describe Aboriginal Canadians. Like "Eskimo," this term has mostly fallen out of use.

Industrial school: Established on and off reservations to train Aboriginal children in trades and to educate and integrate them into white society. Schools typically had a half-day policy where students were expected to attend class for half a day and work during the other half. These schools were government-owned and church-run.

Injustice: A wrongful action taken against an individual or group that denies them their basic rights.

Integration: Combining one group into another, such as a racial, ethnic, or religious group.

Inuit: Aboriginal people who reside in the Canadian Arctic. The Inuit were formerly referred to as "Eskimo."

Metis: French word, meaning "mixed." Aboriginal people of mixed heritage, typically Aboriginal and European.

Native: Being the first people to populate an area. The native Canadians were Aboriginals.

Oppression: The feelings, ideas, or demands of an individual or group of people are not recognized or allowed to be expressed by authorities such as the government, justice system, police, or military.

Potlatch: Meaning "to give" in Chinook. Potlatch celebrates social changes such as births, deaths, marriages, and the appointment of a new chief.

Powwow: Traditionally, a powwow is a ceremony of thanks to Mother Earth for all that she has provided. A powwow includes music and dance.

Prejudice: An attitude, usually negative, directed toward a person or group of people based on wrong or distorted information. Prejudiced thinking may result in acts of discrimination.

Propaganda: The spread of specific information, ideas, or images to control public opinion or actions (such as the residential school video created in the 1950s that showed seemingly happy Aboriginal children at school and put forth the idea that it was in the best interest of the children to attend residential school.

▶ Watch the video at
http://tinyurl.com/rcwresidential066

Racism: A belief that one race is superior to another. People are not treated as equals because of their cultural or ethnic differences. Racism may be systemic (part of institutions, governments, organizations, and programs) or part of the attitudes and behaviour of individuals.

Redress: To right a wrong, sometimes by compensating the victim or by punishing the wrongdoer. Refers to the movement within the Aboriginal community for an official apology and payment for the injustices related to the residential school system

Reserve: Indian reserves were areas of property set aside by the Crown for Aboriginal peoples. Under the *Indian Act*, the Minister of Indian Affairs was given jurisdiction on reserves.

Residential school: Residential schools were boarding schools that were government-owned and church-run. Aboriginal children were taken from their homes and families and sent to these residential schools.

Royal Canadian Mounted Police (RCMP): Also known as the Mounties, these law enforcement officers are known for their red coats and patrolling on horseback.

Segregation: The policy or practice of separating people of different races, classes, or ethnic groups, especially as a form of discrimination.

Sweat lodge: Ceremonial sweat bath used in purification rituals. Sweat lodges are made of natural substances, such as animal skins, stone, and wood.

Treaty: Agreement between two parties. Treaties were drafted by the Crown and the Canadian government to encourage peace and to define the rights of Aboriginal people.

Truth and Reconciliation Commission: The TRC was created to investigate and discover the truth about the treatment of students at the residential schools and to facilitate reconciliation with them.

Tuberculosis: An infection of the lungs that is contagious and may cause death.

Visible minority: This is a modern term used to describe people of an ethnic group who have physical features, usually skin colour, that make them distinct from the majority of the population.

For Further Reading

Books:

Andre, Julie-Ann and Mindy Willett. *We feel good out here = Zhik gwaa'an, nakhwatthaiitat gwiinzii (The Land is Our Storybook).* Fifth House Publishers, 2008.

Bartleman, James. *As Long As The Rivers Flow.* Toronto: Knopf Canada, 2011.

Campbell, Nicola. *Shi-Shi-Etko.* Toronto: Groundwood Books, 2005.

Fontaine, Theodore. *Broken Circle: The Dark Legacy of Indian Residential Schools: A Memoir.* Victoria: Heritage House Publishing, 2010.

Grant, Agnes. *Finding My Talk: How Fourteen Canadian Native Women Reclaimed Their Lives After Residential School.* Toronto: Fitzhenry & Whiteside, 2004.

Hill, Gord. *The 500 Years of Resistance Comic Book.* Vancouver: Arsenal Pulp Press, 2010.

Jordan-Fenton, Christy and Margaret Pokiak-Fenton. *Fatty Legs: A True Story.* Illustrated by Liz Amini-Holmes. Toronto: Annick Press, 2010.

Jordan-Fenton, Christy and Margaret Pokiak-Fenton. *A Stranger At Home.* Illustrated by Liz Amini-Holmes. Toronto: Annick Press, 2011.

Jordan-Fenton, Christy and Margaret Pokiak-Fenton. *When I Was Eight.* Illustrated by Liz Amini-Holmes. Toronto: Annick Press, 2013.

Jordan-Fenton, Christy and Margaret Pokiak-Fenton. *Not My Girl.* Illustrated by Gabrielle Grimard. Toronto: Annick Press, 2014.

Loyie, Larry. *As Long as the Rivers Flow.* Toronto: Groundwood Books, 2005.

Merasty, Joseph Auguste. The Education of Augie Merasty: A Residential School Memoir. Regina: University of Regina Press, 2015.

Olsen, Sylvia, Rita Morris and Ann Sam. *No Time to Say Goodbye: Children's Stories of Kuper Island Residential School.* Winlaw, BC: Sono Nis Press, 2001.

Ralston Saul, Paul. *The Comeback.* Toronto: Penguin Canada, 2014.

Robertson, David Alexander. *7 Generations: A Plains Cree Saga.* Illustrated by Scott B. Henderson. Winnipeg: Highwater Press, 2012.

Robertson, David Alexander. *Sugar Falls: A Residential School Story.* Illustrated by Scott B. Henderson. Winnipeg: Highwater Press, 2012.

Sterling, Shirley. *My Name is Seepeetza.* Toronto: Groundwood Books, 1992.

Wagamese, Richard. *Indian Horse.* Madeira Park, BC: Douglas & McIntyre, 2012.

Films:

Muffins for Granny. Dir. Nadia McLaren. Mongrel Media, 2007. DVD.

Shi-Shi-Etko. Dir. Kate Kroll. 2009. DVD. [Based on the picture book by Nicola Campbell. Available at 1-800-684-3014 or mailbox@movingimages.ca].

We Were Children. Dir. Tim Wolochatiuk. National Film Board, 2012. DVD. [Available at www.nfb.ca/film/we_were_children].

Websites:

www.cbc.ca/news/canada/a-history-of-residential-schools-in-canada-1.702280 — A History of Residential Schools in Canada.

www.irsr.ca — Indian Residential School Resources.

www.legacyofhope.ca — Legacy of Hope Foundation.

www.wherearethechildren.ca — Where Are The Children?

Reference Books:

Daschuk, James. *Clearing the Plains: Disease, Politics of Starvation, and the Loss of Aboriginal Life.* Regina: University of Regina Press, 2013.

Miller, J. R. *Shingwauk's Vision: A History of Native Residential Schools.* Toronto: University of Toronto Press, 1996.

Truth and Reconciliation Commission of Canada. *Final Report of the Truth and Reconciliation Commission of Canada, Volume One: Summary: Honouring the Truth, Reconciling for the Future.* Toronto: James Lorimer & Company Ltd., Publishers, 2015.

Truth and Reconciliation Commission of Canada. "Honouring the Truth, Reconciling for the Future: Summary of the Final Report of the Truth and Reconciliation Commission of Canada." Available online at www.trc.ca/websites/trcinstitution/File/2015/Findings/Exec_Summary_2015_05_31_web_o.pdf.

▶ WATCH THE VIDEO

Look for this symbol throughout the book for links to video and audio clips available online.

Visit www.lorimer.ca/wrongs to see the entire series

Additional books, films, websites, and videos are listed in the Resources section of the Righting Canada's Wrongs series website at www.lorimer.ca/wrongs.

Visual Credits

Every effort has been made to locate the original copyright owners. If the reader has any additional information on the original copyright owners, we would be happy to include it in any revised additions.

Aboriginal Affairs and Northern Development / Affaires autochtones et Developpement du Nord Canada, Communications Branch: p. 101 (top); 119 (top left)

Aboriginal Healing Foundation. *A Healing Journey: Final Report, Summary Points / Cheminement de guérison: points sommaires du rapport final*. Ottawa, 2006: p. 1; p. 83 (bottom right); p. 93 (bottom right); p. 118 (bottom right).

Aboriginal Healing Foundation. *From Truth to Reconciliation: Transforming the Legacy of Residential Schools*. Ottawa, 2008: p. 118 (top right)

Aboriginal Healing Foundation. "The Healing Has Begun – An Operational Update from the AHF": p. 59 (bottom); p. 64 (bottom); p. 89 (bottom)

Aboriginal Healing Foundation. "Response, Responsibility, and Renewal." Ottawa, 2009: p. 80 (middle left and middle right); p. 92 (bottom right); p. 118 (bottom left)

The Aboriginal Multi-Media Society (AMMSA). *Windspeaker*. Edmonton: p. 7; p. 97 (bottom middle); p. 107 (bottom); p. 108 (top and bottom); p. 113; p. 119 (middle left, bottom left, and top right); p. 103

"Addictive Behaviours Among Aboriginal People in Canada." Ottawa: Aboriginal Healing Foundation, 2007: p. 92 (bottom left)

Agnes, Jack. *Behind Closed Doors: Stories from the Kamloops Indian Residential School*. Theytus Books, 2006: p. 49 (bottom right)

Amini-Holmes, Liz: p. 1; p. 7; p. 55 (top); p. 67 (bottom right); p. 74 (top left)

Archives of the Saint-Boniface Historical Society, Oblates of Mary Immaculate of the Province of Manitoba Fonds: p. 73 (top, SHSB 26944)

Assembly of First Nations/First Nations Information Governance Committee.
First Nations Regional Longitudinal Health Survey (RHS) 2002/2003." Ottawa, 2007: p. 92 (top)

Atlantic Policy Congress of First Nations Chiefs: p. 118 (top left); p. 119 (bottom right)

Baldwin, Doug, Rick Mahoney, Don Quinlan, Kevin Reed. Edited by Elaine Aboud and Loralee Case. *The Canadian Challenge*. Oxford University Press, 2008: p. 95 (top, middle left)

Barlow, Kevin J. *Residential Schools, Prisons and HIV/AIDS Among Aboriginal People in Canada: Exploring the Connections*: p. 89 (middle right)

Best Start: Ontario Maternal, Newborn and Early Development Resource Centre. "A Sense of Belonging: Supporting Healthy Child Development in Aboriginal Families." Toronto, 2006: p. 93 (top left)

Blackman, Diana: p. 87 (bottom left)

Blondin-Perrin, Alice. *My Heart Shook Like a Drum – What I Learned at the Indian Mission Schools, Northwest Territories*. Borealis Press, 2009: p. 73 (left); p. 86 (right); p. 90 (right)

Chambers, Steve. *This Is Your Church: A Guide to the Beliefs, Policies, and Positions of the United Church of Canada*. United Church Pub House, 1993: p. 104 (right).

Churchill, Ward. *Kill the Indian, Save the Man: The Genocidal Impact of American Indian Residential Schools*: p. 54 (left); p. 64 (top); p. 80 (top)

Densmore, Frances. *How Indians Use Wild Plants for Food, Medicine & Crafts*. Dover Publications, 1974: p. 13 (top)

Dickson, Olive Patricia. *Canada's First Nations: a history of founding peoples from earliest times*. Oxford University Press, 2001: p. 16 (bottom right)

Ennamorato, Judith. *Sing the Brave Song*. Raven Press, 1998: p. 40 (top)

Fairbairn, Douglas H. *A Nation Beckons: Canada 1896–1914*. Prentice-Hall of Canada, 1987: p. 15 (bottom); p. 40 (bottom)

Flowers, Marjorie: p. 49 (bottom left)

Fontaine, Theodore. *Broken Circle: The Dark Legacy of Indian Residential Schools*. Heritage House Publishing, 2010: p. 53 (middle); p. 73 (bottom right); p. 74 (top right); p. 81 (top right); p. 88 (top left)

Fontaine, Phil: p. 101 (bottom); p. 102

General Motors: p. 20 (top right); p. 35 (top and bottom right)

The General Synod Archives, Anglican Church of Canada: p. 81 (middle left, P7538-187); p. 85 (bottom right, P75-103-S7-151); p. 104 (top left).

Glenbow Museum Archives: p. 8 (right NA-1406-40), p. 16 (bottom left, NA-1338-102); p. 39 (bottom, NA-1480-31); p. 41 (bottom, NC-5-8); p. 44 (top, NA-3170); p. 75 (top right, NA-1934-1); p.82 (bottom, NA-4212-42); p. 83 (top, M-9028-27; bottom left, PA-2807-3403); p. 85 (top, M-9028-461)

Globe & Mail: p. 99 (bottom right)

Government of Northwest Territories, Government of Nunavut, and the Legacy of Hope Foundation. "The Residential School System in Canada: Understanding the Past — Seeking Reconciliation — Building Hope for Tomorrow," Second Edition. 2013: p. 11 (bottom right); p. 18 (bottom right); p. 19 (top right); p. 37 (bottom)

Grant, Agnes. *Finding My Talk: How Fourteen Canadian Native Women Reclaimed their Lives after Residential School*. Fifth House Publishers, 2004: p. 97 (top left)

A Healing Journey: p. 83 (bottom right); p. 93 (bottom right); p. 118 (bottom right)

Highwater, Jamake. *Ritual of the Wind*. Toronto: Methuen Publications, 1984: p. 31 (bottom); p. 35 (bottom left)

Highway, Tomson. *The Rez Sisters*. Saskatoon: Fifth House Publishers, 1988: p. 96 (bottom left)

Hudson's Bay Company Archives, Archives of Manitoba: p. 1 (HBCA 1987/363-G-102/11

Illustrated History of Canada's Native People: p. 7; p. 9 (bottom right); p. 10 (middle); p. 12 (right); p. 13 (bottom); p. 14 (middle left); p. 17 (top right and bottom right); p. 20 (bottom right); p. 21 (top and bottom); p. 22 (top); p. 26 (bottom); p. 27 (top; middle right); p. 28 (top left, top right); p. 29 (top, bottom left and bottom right); p. 32 (top); p. 33 (bottom left and middle right); p. 34 (middle right); p. 39 (top); p. 40 (middle); p. 41 (top); p. 42 (right); p. 43 (bottom); p. 72 (left); p. 77 (bottom right); p. 90 (right); p. 96 (bottom right)

Jordan-Fenton, Christy and Pokaik-Fenton, Margaret. *A Stranger at Home*. Annick Press, 2011: p. 86 (left)

Kabotie, Fred. Courtesy of the School of American Research, Santa Fe, NM: p. 36 (top left).

Kallen, Stuart A. *Indian Gaming*. Michigan: Thompson Gale, 2006: p. 91 (top right)

Knockwood, Isabelle. *Out of the Depths*. Roseway Publishing, 2001: p. 55 (middle right); p. 81 (middle right)

Langevin, Hector. *They Came for the Children*. The Truth and Reconciliation Commission of Canada, 2012: p. 28 (bottom); p. 30 (middle); p. 37 (top left, top right); p. 59 (top); p. 60 (left); p. 62 (top left and bottom); p. 66 (top left); p. 67 (bottom left); p. 68 (bottom); p. 76 (top); p. 81 (top left); p. 84 (top left); p. 94 (top and bottom); p. 100

Library and Archives Canada: p. 1 (R12671-9-7-E); p. 1 (PA-101771); p. 7 (C-37113), p. 8 (right, NA-1406-40; left, C-040293); p. 9 (top left, C-010513); p. 12 (left, C-001024); p. 14 (top left); p. 17 (bottom left, PA-182268); p. 20 (left, C-114374k); p. 24 (bottom left, PA-059608; top right, e003894485; bottom right, C-040293); p. 25 (middle right, PA-188612); p. 26 (top, C-024283; middle left, C-024278; middle right, C-002263); p. 32 (bottom left, PA-181728; bottom right); p. 36 (bottom right, PA-044554); p. 38 (bottom, e008299871); p. 39 (middle, PA-102086); p. 43 (top left, C-006536; top right, PA-010657); p. 45 (bottom, PA-050799); p. 47 (top); p. 50 (left, PA-040715; right, e008440682); p. 51 (top, C-000321; middle, PA-101542); p. 54 (right, PA-195124); p. 56 (top left, PA-010634; top right, PA-182251); p. 57 (top right, PA-134110; bottom left, PA-210885; bottom right, e010765703); p. 60 (right, PA-042133); p. 61 (right, PA-185530); p. 63 (bottom PA-185528); p. 65 (top right, PA-101771); p. 66 (top right, PA-185879); p. 69 (top left); p. 74 (bottom, e010968993); p. 75 (bottom left, PA-166582; bottom right, e002504650); p. 77 (top left, PA-181590; bottom left, PA-195125); p. 78 (bottom right, e006610161; bottom left, PA-023091); p. 79 (top right, PA-185653; middle left, PA-185534); p. 82 (top, PA-048570); p. 85 (bottom left, PA-212560); p. 96 (top); p. 98 (e000008950)

Llewellyn, Jennifer. "Bridging the Gap between Truth and Reconciliation: Restorative Justice and the Indian Residential School Truth and Reconciliation Commission." 2008: p. 106 (bottom).

Macdonald, Robert. *The Romance of Canadian History. Canada III, The Uncharted Nation*. The Ballantrae Foundation. Vancouver: Evergreen Press Ltd.,: 1978: p. 9 (top right)

Manitoba Museum of Man and Nature EP 4233: p. 51 (bottom)

Marston, Ashley: p. 109 (top)

Miller, J.R. *Shingwauk's Vision*. University of Toronto Press, Scholarly Publishing Division, 1996: p. 17 (top left); p. 18 (top); p. 30 (top); p. 34 (top and bottom left); p. 42 (left); p. 47 (bottom); p. 52 (left and right); p. 53 (top); p. 58 (top and bottom); p. 65 (bottom right); p. 66 (bottom); p. 67 (top right); p. 76 (bottom left hand middle right); p. 78 (top left and top right); p. 79 (top left and bottom right)

Milloy, John S. *A National Crime*. University of Manitoba Press, 1999: p. 61 (left, MMMn EP 692); p. 62 (top right)

The Missionary Oblates of Mary Immaculate: p. 105 (top left).

The Mounties and Law Enforcement: p. 48 (left)

Museum of Canadian History: p. 16 (top, D2005-09796)

Nashville Predators: p. 97 (bottom left)

The Newberry Library, Chicago: p. 33 (top right)

Ontario Archives: p. 72 (right, 10005190); p. 84 (top right, 10022955; bottom, 10022957); p. 85 (middle right, 10022834); p. 89 (top, 10005419)

Ottawa, Gilles. *Pensionnats Indiens au Quebec Undouble Regard*. Cornac, 2010: p. 1; p. 45 (top); p. 53 (bottom); p. 81 (bottom left); p. 97 (bottom right)

Patterson, Colleen: p. 115

Penn, W.S. *The Telling of the World: Native American stories and art*. Stewart Tabori & Chang, 1996: p. 1; p. 36 (top right); p. 87 (top left, top right)

Ramen Fred. *Native American Mythology*. The Rosen Publishing Group Inc., 2008: p. 14 (middle right); p. 18 (bottom left); p. 30 (bottom); p. 31 (top)

Rasky, Frank. *The Taming of the Canadian West*. Toronto: McClellend and Stewart, 1967: p. 9 (bottom left)

The RCMP: p. 49 (top)

Richardson, Boyce. *People of Terra Nullius*. General Publishing Co., 1994: p. 46 (left)

Saskatchewan Archives Board: p. 56 (bottom left, R-82239(1); bottom right, R-82239(2))

Shutterstock: p. 105 (right)

Telling the World: p. 36 (top right)

Ternier, Irene. *People of the Fur Trade – From Native Trappers to Chief Factors*. Toronto: Heritage House Publishing, 2011: p. 23 (top); p. 46 (right)

Terrace Standard: p. 95 (middle right).

Toronto Star: p. 99 (June 12, 2008).

Truth and Reconciliation Commission Quebec National Event Program – 2013: p. 106 (top right); p. 107 (middle); p. 109 (bottom right)

We Were So Away: The Inuit Experience of Residential Schools. Legacy of Hope Foundation, 2010: p. 1; p. 10 (top left); p. 15 (top); p. 19 (top left and bottom right); p. 22 (bottom left and bottom right); p. 44 (bottom); p. 48 (right); p. 65 (bottom left); p. 68 (top); p. 69 (top right and bottom); p. 70 (top left, top right, and bottom); p. 71 (top right and bottom); p. 88 (middle left, bottom right); p. 91 (bottom left); p. 97 (top right)

Williams, Shirley: p. 55 (middle left)

Yukon Archives: p. 7 (T-127)

Index

A

Abikoki, Jim 41
Acoose, Janice 65
Act to Encourage the Gradual Civilization of Indian Tribes 38, 42
alcohol 20, 21, 22, 44, 45, 48, 50, 87, 90, 91, 92, 95
American Revolution 36, 41
Annett, Kevin 75
Assembly of First Nations 94, 100, 117
Assiniboine 20
August, George 107

B

Basile, Jacqueline 81
Battiste, Harriette 77
bedwetting 74
Belcourt, Christi 119
Bellegarde, Perry 117
Bernard, Nora 66, 74, 94
Biedermann, Kyleigh 92
Bisson, Cassandra 92
Blackman, Diana 87
Blondin, Alice 73, 86, 90
Blue Quills Native Education Council 84
Bone, Emily 79
Brant, Joseph. *See* Thayendanegea
Bryce, P. H. 81

C

Cachagee, Mike 100
Cardinal, Harold 85
carpentry 60
ceremonies (traditional) 27, 29, 46, 48, 83, 92. *See also* potlatches; powwows; Sun Dances; sweat lodges
Charlie, Rose Dorothy 61
Chrétien, Jean 83, 84, 85
churches 24, 30, 31, 37, 45, 48, 63, 64, 82, 94, 102, 104–105, 111, 112, 118
Clelaman (chief) 46
clothing (residential school) 54, 55, 56, 66, 102, 111
clothing (traditional) 10, 12, 16, 17, 22, 25, 33
colonization 12, 110, 111, 117
Cree 15, 17, 20, 77, 78, 83
Crowchild, Dave 82
Crowfoot 39
cultural genocide 110, 111

D

dancing 24, 26, 27, 29, 37, 46, 92. *See also* ceremonies; Sun Dances
day schools 82, 83, 84, 85, 90
dental care 75
Department of Indian Affairs 42, 43, 58, 82, 83, 85, 97, 101
divorce
dogs 16, 17, 19, 33, 71
Doucette, Dorothy 75

Douglas, Amelia 47
Douglas, James 47
drums 29. *See also* ceremonies

E

education (traditional) 24, 31, 32–37
Elias, Lillian 49, 91
enfranchisement 42, 45
European settlers 8, 11, 13, 14, 15, 18, 20, 21, 38

F

farming (residential school) 60, 66
farming (traditional) 9, 12, 18
Ferrier (reverend) 37
fires (residential schools) 64, 80, 81
Flower, Marjorie 49, 52, 69
Flowers, Shirley 71, 91
Fontaine, Phil 94, 95, 100, 101, 104, 105
Fontaine, Theodore 52, 62, 73, 74, 88
food (residential school) 54, 58, 70, 76
fur trading 11, 15, 17, 18, 20, 21, 23
fishing 8, 9, 10, 12, 14, 20, 32, 34, 58, 85

G

Gillespie, Kate 76
Gregoire, Edna 76

H

hair (significance of) 17, 54
haircuts 54, 55
Harper, Stephen 101, 103, 116
Highway, Tomson 96
homelessness 87
Hubbard-Rudulovich, Hanako 92
Hudson's Bay Company 10, 18, 20, 22, 39
hunting 8, 9, 10, 12, 17, 18, 19, 20, 21, 22, 25, 30, 32, 33, 34, 35, 40, 71, 85. *See also* over-hunting
Huron 40

I

ice fishing 10. *See also* fishing
Idle No More 97
illnesses (at residential schools) 75, 80, 81
Indian Act 37, 44, 45, 46, 48, 68, 82, 83, 97, 117
Indian agent 45, 46, 48
Indian Residential School Settlement Agreement (IRS) 94, 98, 103, 106, 115, 116, 119

Indian Residential School Survivors Society 94
infants 24, 25, 32
Institute for Advancement of Aboriginal Women 119
Inuit Tapiriit Kanatami 100
Irniq, Peter 56, 64, 69, 70, 88, 100
Iroquois 9, 12, 13, 22, 26, 36, 40
Isapo-muxika. *See* Crowfoot

J

Jacobs, Beverly 100
Joe, Rita 67, 78
Johnson, Lottie May 115
Jordan, Judy 78
Jordan-Fenton, Christy 55
Joseph, Martha 73, 95
Joseph, Robert 94

K

Knockwood, Isabelle 35, 51, 55, 57, 63, 67, 76, 77
Knockwood, Rosie 55, 57
Kutcha-Kutchi 26

L

languages (European) 37, 54, 57
languages (First Nations, Inuit, and Metis) 8, 10, 24, 28, 32, 37, 38, 54, 57, 63, 72, 74, 78, 86, 96, 102, 104, 110, 111, 112, 117
Littlechild, George 83
Littlechild, Wilton 107
Loft, Frederick 58
Longboat, Tom 96

M

Macdonald, John A. 42, 111
MacDonald, Velma 69
Mackenzie and Yukon River Basin First Nations 9
malnutrition 58–59, 73, 82
Manuel, George 58, 85
Marble, Nancy 75
Marston, Luke 109
Mass (religious ceremony) 60, 64, 65, 66
McLachlin, Beverley 111
McLean, Lachlan 79
medicines (traditional) 12, 14
Merasty, Crystal 100
migration 8, 9, 16, 17
Mi'kmaq 8, 34, 38, 67, 75, 119

missionaries 24, 30, 31, 32, 68, 90
Mohawk 36, 41
monuments 115, 118–119
Moonias, Mary 100
Moore, P. E. 58
Moore, Thomas 56
Mulcair, Tom 117

N

National Council for Reconciliation 114
National Day of Action 95
Niviaxie, Carolyn 71
Northern Plains 35
North-West Rebellion 39
Nuu-chah-nulth 14

O

Ojibwa 18, 32
over-hunting 15

P

Pacific Coast First Nations 8, 9, 20, 47
Papequash, Campbell 54
Paul, Betsey 75
pets 25, 33
physical abuse 57, 72, 75, 90, 94, 95, 102, 104
Plains First Nations 9, 15, 20, 35
Pokiak-Fenton, Margaret 55
post-traumatic stress disorder 87
potlatches 28 , 46, 47
Poundmaker (chief) 15
poverty 87, 89, 90, 95, 97, 110, 111
powwows 26, 27, 97
prostitution 87
psychological abuse 86, 88, 90, 94

Q

Quick-to-See Smith, Jaune 87
Quirt, Bessie 68

R

Raciette, Adeline 79
Red Paper 85
Red Sky (chief) 37
Reed, Hayter 43
reserves 15, 16, 30, 39, 40, 41, 42, 45, 48, 80, 82, 85, 111
Riel, Louis 39
Royal Canadian Mounted Police (RCMP) 48, 98
Ruben, Abraham 90

Rudstad, John 116
runaways 48, 74, 80, 81

S

Salish 17, 33, 109
Scott, Duncan Campbell 43
sexual abuse 72, 73, 87, 94, 95, 102, 104, 107, 111
shelters (traditional) 8, 9, 16–18, 71
Shot Both Sides, Jim 83
Siksika 39
Simon, Mary 100
Sinclair, Murray 106, 107, 109, 119
Smith, Agnes 97
Soop, Everett 83
Stevens, Irene 108
suicide 80, 87, 95, 97
Sun Dances 16, 46
sweat lodges 14, 26, 30, 119

T

Thayendanegea 36, 41
Tootoo, Jordin 97
Tootoo, Terence 97
totem poles 26
trading 14, 16, 18, 20–23, 27, 29. *See also* fur trade
transportation (traditional) 16, 18, 19
trapping 8, 12
treaties 15, 38, 39, 40, 42, 44, 83, 110, 111, 114, 115, 117
truant officers 48
Trudeau, Justin 116, 117
Trudeau, Pierre Elliot 85
Truth and Reconciliation Commission (TRC) 98, 103, 106–109, 110, 111, 112, 113, 115, 116
Tsimshian 26
Tsuu T'ina 30
Tungilik, Marius 88, 97

V

Vankoughnet, Lawrence 42, 43
Venne, Rachelle 119

W

weapons 8, 22, 25, 32, 33
Williams, Shirley 55, 61, 83
Wilson, Marie 107, 109
Woodland First Nations 8, 12
Wynne, Kathleen 117

Y

Yellowfly, Teddy 82
Young, Phil 87
Yuxweluptun, Lawrence Paul 40